SM9 800 8447

KU-266-873

HJH P
(Spe)

PROMOTING COMMUNITY HEALTH

Developing the role of local government

LANCASTER

075 211 4484

PROMOTING COMMUNITY HEALTH

Developing the role of local government

Viv Speller
Wessex Institute for Health Research and Development

Project team
Antony Morgan, HEA
John Johnson, LGMB
Tricia Younger, HEA
Moira Kelly, HEA
Rhiannon Barker, HEA
Viv Speller, WIHRD

ISBN 0 7521 1448 4
© Health Education Authority, 1999
Health Education Authority
Trevelyan House
30 Great Peter Street
London SW1P 2HW
Printed in Great Britain

Contents

Social capital for health Preface to the series   vii

Executive summary   ix

1. Introduction   1

2. Method   5

3. Quality of life   12

4. Poverty and inequalities   16

5. Working with the community   22

6. Joint working and relationships   32

7. Developing joint health strategies   40

8. Health for All 2000 and Health of the Nation   45

9. Political influence and accountability   50

10. Measuring success   55

11. Discussion   59

References   67

Social capital for health
Preface to the series

The recently published Acheson Report on Inequalities in Health and the Government's public health strategy 'Our Healthier Nation', recognise that the solutions to major public health problems such as heart disease, cancers, mental health and accidents are complex. They will require interventions which cut across sectors to take account of the broader social, cultural, economic, political and physical environments which shape people's experiences of health and wellbeing.

A major challenge is how to influence these broader determinants of health in such a way that relative inequalities in health can be addressed.

Recent evidence suggests that social approaches to the organisation and delivery of public health may have considerable potential for health improvement, particularly for those that suffer most disadvantage in society. The evidence base for moving forward in this field is, however, somewhat limited.

The Health Education Authority is committed to developing this evidence base and to testing social approaches to reducing health inequalities and to the promotion of health and the prevention of disease.

The HEA's first Research Strategy 1996–99 initiated a programme to investigate the concept of social capital and to establish the empirical links between aspects of social capital such as trust, reciprocity, local democracy, citizenship, civic engagement, social relationships, social support, and health outcomes, access to services, information and to power.

Social capital serves as one coherent construct which will allow us to progress the debate and discussion about the general importance of social approaches to public health and health promotion. It is however only one part of an approach to health improvement, which must also clearly embrace structural changes.

The HEA's new programme of Social Action Research in two city sites will build upon the evidence produced thus far, to demonstrate the effectiveness of a range of integrated social approaches, implemented through collaborative initiatives by local authorities, health authorities and the voluntary sector.

The early work on social capital will also feed into new in-depth analyses of social networks and citizen power and their importance to health by gender, age, ethnicity and further explore its relationships to health and inequality in individuals and in populations.

Over the coming year the HEA will be publishing a series of reports summarising the initial results of the exploratory work on social capital and its links to health.

This first report presents findings from a small qualitative study carried out with representatives from local authorities. Using the concept of social capital as a framework for discussion, the research explores the potential for local authorities to contribute to the new health agenda through direct action, and partnerships and alliances with other organisations.

Professor Pamela Gillies
Director of Research
Health Education Authority

Executive summary

During the autumn/winter of 1997/98 twenty-eight directors and senior managers of local authority departments, from rural districts to urban boroughs in England, were interviewed about their current approaches to promoting health in their communities and potential for further action. The study aimed to explore their attitudes to working to promote health both within their departments and in partnership with other agencies, and the barriers and opportunities they perceived. Topics discussed included health promotion actions, interdepartmental and interagency partnerships, and their contribution to improving the quality of life and developing 'social capital' in communities.

Interviewees were drawn from chief executive, education, environmental health, housing, leisure and social services departments. Interviews were tape-recorded, transcribed and analysed using Ethnograph. The results are discussed under the headings of quality of life, poverty and inequalities, working with the community, joint working and relationships, priorities and strategies, Health for All 2000 and Health of the Nation, political influence and accountability, and ways of measuring success.

Local authorities felt that they had a responsibility to promote the quality of life, and were in a better position to influence this than health authorities. Poor quality of life was associated with ill-health, and both housing and social services departments targeted the deprived or at-risk. Leisure and tourism contributed to the quality of the environment and the economy of the area to support positive health and well-being. However, contacts between services and the poorer sections of the community were not always used to consider wider health needs and interviewees felt that health authorities were not as interested in health inequalities. Concerns were also expressed about the negative consequences of short-term initiatives to target inequalities. Provision of advice services tended to be reactive to health concerns, and health issues did not seem to figure prominently in bids for economic regeneration.

Local authorities have developed a variety of solutions such as community action forums, local ward committees and advisory panels to understand the needs of their communities in order to provide more responsive services, and to develop self-esteem and self-sustaining communities. Although community development approaches were valued there appeared to be little co-ordination between these and other mechanisms for community engagement. While these mechanisms addressed environmental health and quality of life issues they were rarely used to consider other health and health service concerns. It is suggested that health authorities should consider ways of sharing these approaches with local authorities rather than establishing separate methods of community consultation.

Many problems with joint working between health and local authorities were cited including structural, organisational and perceptual differences. Interviewees expressed concern that health representatives paid more attention to treatment rather than prevention. Links with primary care were poorly developed, and it was felt that there was little understanding of the role of the political dimension in local authorities that caused tensions. Most were, however, optimistic about progress towards joint health strategies but emphasised the need for a pragmatic approach towards developing practical and achievable joint action plans. There was support for the possibility of shared budgets and a desire to share information particularly with public health departments.

Health for All and Healthy City projects helped to put health on the agenda of the local authority and encouraged joint working between departments, but the individual behavioural focus of Health of the Nation had had a negative effect on some joint working. Generally connections between these initiatives, anti-poverty strategies, Local Agenda 21 and community engagement processes were not well made. Greatest collaboration was seen to have occurred where there were tangible projects with visible outcomes, and there was an understanding that developing alliances took time and effort but that it did bring benefits. From the experiences of successful partnerships and the concerns expressed, it is suggested that health and local authorities and other partners should focus their joint work explicitly in two different types of partnership. Client-focused partnerships would address health inequalities by targeting the work of health, social services and housing onto a common client base. Education would also have a significant role with respect to special needs, educational welfare and school exclusions. Population-focused partnerships would address the wider health concerns and health promotion of geographically defined communities. Key players here would be environmental health, education and leisure services. The NHS would have a significant role through public health information, health promotion services, and primary care, but it is suggested that it is not a lead role. This structure might clarify the proposed health leadership roles for health and local authorities indicated in recent government policy.

Whilst interviewees' theoretical understanding of the construct of social capital was limited there were many indications that they embraced approaches to improving residents' sense of community and quality of life, and were actively pursuing policies and practices that could lead to the building of social capital. However, there was frequently a lack of congruence between community engagement processes and explicit intentions to empower communities. There are potential avenues available through primary care groups and Healthy Living Centres to pull some of this together and draw in the NHS, but at the time of the study there was little evidence that local authorities had been engaged in these processes. The attributes of social capital building are also seen to be relevant to the building of partnerships, which thrived when based on trust, expectations of reciprocity of actions and strong networks of contacts and information sharing.

Local authorities have much to contribute to the promotion of community health but in order to develop this potential the health service needs to understand their unique contributions more clearly to enable all parties to contribute to health promoting partnerships effectively.

1. Introduction

This study was commissioned by the Health Education Authority in 1997 in collaboration with the Local Government Management Board to investigate the potential for health promotion at local government level, using the concept of social capital as a framework for action. An earlier survey of local authorities to find out the nature and extent of their health promotion work identified many examples of health promotion activity (Moran, 1996). It also described a number of barriers to health promotion, including lack of training and funding for initiatives, and limitations on joint working with health authorities. The current study aims to explore more deeply the attitudes and perceptions of senior local authority officers about their roles in promoting community health, based on their experiences in promoting health both through their own service delivery mechanisms and in partnership with other departments and agencies. The fieldwork was conducted during the autumn and winter of 1997/98, which was a period of substantial shift in policy directions from central government, with the publication of the White Paper, *The new NHS* (Department of Health, 1997), the anticipation of the Green Paper, *Our healthier nation* (Department of Health, 1998a), and the consultation paper, *Modernising local government: local democracy and community leadership* (Department of the Environment, Transport and the Regions, 1998a). In addition there were consultation documents in this period on the role of public health, from the Chartered Institute of Environmental Health Officers, *Agendas for change* (Environmental Health Commission, 1997) and the Chief Medical Officer's report on the future of public health (Department of Health, 1998b). The policy shifts towards greater involvement in partnerships and increased focus on health promotion had engendered considerable debate and thought about the implications for future service provision, and the discussions were able to capture much of this reflection on past difficulties and hopes for the future.

Interviews were conducted with senior officers in five local authorities in England, representing the range of types of local council from rural district to urban borough. To assess the opportunities and barriers to local authorities in promoting health three main areas were discussed: health promotion actions; interdepartmental and interagency partnerships; and the contribution made to developing healthy communities by drawing on the concept of social capital. The earlier study (Moran, 1996), and a more recent survey on the health-promoting role of local government in Wales (Roberts and Griffiths, 1998), demonstrate the conceptual difficulties in discussing health promotion with local authorities. For many the term 'health promotion' is translated as meaning specific health promotion activities relating to lifestyle or individual health behaviour change. Thus it is often viewed in the context of projects that are within the remit of health promotion departments. Although the accepted definitions of the scope of health promotion, as in the *Ottawa Charter* (World Health Organization, 1986) and the *Jakarta Declaration* (World Health Organization, 1997) are much wider than this, actions in the spheres of social and environmental health may not be viewed as health promotion. In order to broaden the scope of this enquiry into the ways in which local authorities promote health in the course of their statutory functions as well as in partnerships with others, the phraseology of 'promoting community health' was used. In this way the enquiry was able to penetrate more deeply into the wide range of local authority functions that have an impact on health. It was envisaged that some respondents may have a limited understanding of the social and environmental determinants of health and the links between aspects of their work and community health, but this was not the case, as will be seen in the presentation of the findings. The local authority officers interviewed were very well informed and aware of the potential of their actions for health and critical of the various constraints preventing them from fulfilling it.

Alliances or partnerships to promote health have been shown to work, in terms of enabling action to be taken on the broader determinants of health and wellbeing and on individual health-related behaviour (Gillies, 1998). Within such partnerships the extent to which the community is involved in planning and implementing the approaches also appears to have an impact on their success. This study explored the ways in which local authorities had worked and were planning to work in partnerships, and how they engaged with their local community in health-related activities, as key elements of a successful approach to health promotion. Thus the focus was less on the types of issues and topics addressed, and more on the health-promoting processes used to address them.

Recognising that local authorities are not homogeneous bodies, it is important to acknowledge the complex sets of interrelationships that may be required to promote community health. These do not necessarily always mean partnerships along a health and local authority axis. Joint work with other local authority departments, sometimes across organisations, such as between county and district councils, can be as important and as difficult to maintain. Similarly, joint working with health requires partnerships across and between health authorities, NHS trusts and primary care at both strategic and fieldworker levels. The study aimed to investigate the different types of partnerships that existed, where they worked well in achieving health gain objectives and where there were gaps and problems. It also aimed to understand more about the reasons for success and failure from an individual and service perspective. The experiences of working in established health alliances informed part of these discussions, but other joint working arrangements, formal and informal were also considered.

The research also aimed to explore the potential for building healthier communities by using the concept of social capital. Social capital has been defined by Putnam *et al.* (1994) as the 'features of social life – networks, norms and trust – that enable participants to act together to pursue shared objectives'. Social capital is considered to be a resource that resides in the community at large which can be drawn upon by individuals and groups. It is characterised by civic identity and engagement, trust and reciprocity of actions and networking between individuals, groups and agencies. Putnam's work described a civic community as one where there would be high turnout to vote at local elections, active participation in sports and cultural associations and high local newspaper readership, indicating a degree of interest in and participation in community and civic life by residents. Subsequent studies have linked measures of social capital with health indices and found that there is a correlation between good health and social capital (Wilkinson, 1996; Kawachi *et al.*, 1996; Higgins *et al.*, 1996). Thus the focus was to understand how local authorities viewed their role in terms of developing social capital, or related and perhaps more familiar concepts of 'promoting a sense of community' and 'quality of life', and to explore the potential for developing such avenues in the future.

Consideration of the ways in which local authorities engaged with their local community related particularly to these roles in developing a sense of community and improving quality of life, but also underpinned other aspects of discussions, such as improving service delivery, determining priorities and accountability issues. The study aimed to explore the different methods local authorities were using to involve their local communities in the activities of the council, such as service consultations, needs assessment, community development and empowerment; and to consider to what extent these mechanisms were, and could be, used for health improvement and building social capital.

This study aimed to understand more about the different ways in which local authority officers perceive health, and how they feel it may be improved. The emphasis was to illuminate their visions of a healthier future and ways of achieving it that go beyond current joint activity and alliances in order to harness the considerable and essential potential of local authorities in this endeavour. Thus the focus was on searching for ways in which they are, and can continue, contributing to the promotion and maintenance of health that are congruent with their current and developing roles and activities. While many of the messages in this report may not be new, the depth of feeling and similarity of experience across departments in different types of councils in different parts of the country lend credence to the findings. Those involved in developing partnerships and promoting community health should acknowledge the considerable potential for local authorities to improve health and enhance social capital when working in synergy across departments and agencies.

Since the interviews were done the government has issued a wealth of policy guidance on these issues. The White Paper *Modern local government: in touch with the people* (Department of the Environment, Transport and the Regions, 1998b) describes the modern council as leaders of their community, organising and supporting partnerships, involving and responding to local people. To improve local democracy they will have a duty to consult and engage with local communities and 'consultation and participation should be embedded into the culture of all councils' (para. 4.6). In addition new legislation will place on councils a duty to promote the economic, social and environmental wellbeing of their areas (para 8.8).

Partnership in action (new opportunities for joint working between health and social services) (Department of Health, 1998c) was launched for consultation in September 1998. This plans to make partnerships between health and social services the norm rather than the exception through the removal of legislative and historical barriers to joint working. This would be evidenced at three levels: strategic planning, service commissioning and service provision. The report *Bringing Britain together: a national strategy for neighbourhood renewal* (Social Exclusion Unit, 1998) was also presented to government in September 1998 with proposals on integrated and sustainable approaches to the problems of the worst housing estates, including crime, drugs, unemployment, community breakdown and bad schools. All of these approaches will have a substantial impact on the areas reviewed in the scope of this study, and will depend on the skills and capacities of local government officers, in partnership with colleagues in health and with their communities, to achieve the substantial shifts in practice and outcomes required. This study provides an insight into the readiness of local authorities to move in these directions and the challenges they anticipate. In particular it emphasises throughout the attention that needs to be paid to the relationships required between health and local authorities to promote community health and wellbeing.

2. Method

Data collection and analysis

This was a small-scale study that attempted to maximise the depth of enquiry by using semi-structured interviews to penetrate deeply the thoughts and aspirations of interviewees in a limited number of areas in a 'safe' environment where anonymity was assured. This report is based on the analysis of transcriptions of interviews conducted with senior officers in five local authorities. The authorities represented: a new unitary authority in an urban city; a district council covering a rural area with a city, small towns and villages; a county council; a metropolitan city council; and a London borough. The first two covered parts of their local health authority area, the county covered three health authorities, the metropolitan city council was coterminous with the health authority, and the London borough covered half of the health authority area. The sampling strategy aimed to maximise variety to ensure generalisability to a range of local authority and departmental types, rather than to be statistically representative.

A contact in each local authority, in some cases known to the researcher, was approached to seek permission for their involvement in the study. Usually this was referred to a senior officer to obtain approval and identification of key officers at director or assistant director level in each department, representing housing, environmental health, social services, education and leisure. Officers were approached to arrange interviews of about one hour. It had been hoped to include the views of elected members in this enquiry, as local government officers work in a political context, but owing to constraints of time it was not possible to gain access to busy councillors. One interview did however include a committee chair.

Interviews

Twenty-four interviews were conducted in the five authorities, comprising 28 interviewees. One interview was lost to the analysis owing to failure in the recording equipment. Interviews were with director, assistant director or other senior manager in each authority. Interviewees were assured anonymity with respect to both their authority and themselves in the publication of the findings. Quotations are identified by an alphanumeric code denoting departmental type and respondent number. Although departmental groupings and descriptions varied between the authorities, the number of interviewees in each broad category of service is given in Table 1.

Table 1. Interviews by service group

Service group	No. of interviews	No. of interviewees
Leisure (L)	4	4
Housing (H)	6	7
Social services (S)	3	4*
Environmental health (E)	5	5
Chief executive/corporate (X)	2	2
Education (D)	3	5
Total	**23**	**27**

*Included chair of social services committee

A semi-structured interview schedule was prepared and revised after the experience of the first four interviews to shorten it and focus more clearly on key issues. However, the content of the schedule was not significantly changed, and the first interviews were retained in the analysis. The interview schedule (see appendix) opened with discussion of the role of the interviewee and their department, and their considerations of the extent to which their work contributed to the promotion of health. This covered both strategic and operational aspects, and examples of particular projects where offered. Methods of involving the community in assessing needs and planning the delivery of local services were discussed. The links between the department and healthy city or Health for All (HFA) projects in the locality were considered, as well as other aspects of joint work with the health service. Discussion of the main determinants of health was interwoven into these responses and rarely needed prompting. Specific attention was paid to the role of the local authority in economic development and in addressing inequalities. The theme of the local authority's role in developing social capital was introduced and discussion turned around the concepts of developing a 'sense of community' and promoting the 'quality of life'. The ways in which the success of specific projects and of less tangible goals of the authority were measured were also considered. The interviews concluded with reflection on the reviews of the Health of the Nation and of the future role of public health and what the respondents would like to see coming out of these.

All the interviews were tape-recorded and subsequently transcribed and entered into Ethnograph (v4) for coding. Coding was done by the interviewer and a code list was generated. These codes were grouped by the major themes emerging from the interviews (see Table 2).

Table 2. Codes and definitions

Main theme	Code	Definition
Services	access	access to services
	commdevt	community development
	education	education department
	envtserv	environmental health department
	housing	housing department
	leisserv	leisure services
	pubhlth	public health/preventive services
	socserv	social services
	tradstand	trading standards
Health issues	disabil	disabilities, physical and learning
	environt	environmental issues
	inequal	inequalities
	hivaids	HIV/AIDS and sexual health
	lifestyles	general lifestyles and health behaviour
	mentalill	mental ill health
	mentalprom	mental health promotion
	parenting	quality of parenting
	physact	physical activity, exercise
	poverty	poverty
	safety	health and safety, accident prevention
	smoking	smoking and smoking cessation
	subsmis	substance misuse
	transport	transport and mobility
Population groups	children	children and adolescents
	adults	adults
	oldpeople	older people, retired
Resources	budgets	departmental resources
	contracts	contracts, specifications for services
	discount	discount schemes, incentives
	economy	economy of the area
	econregen	economic regeneration, SRB bids
	purchase	purchasing or commissioning role
Community	commaction	community action forums, groups, etc.
	comminform	knowledge and information, use of and by
	commsaf	community safety
	needsasst	needs assessment, priority identification
	networks	community networks and support
	nimby	not in my back yard – protectionism
	quallife	quality of life
	userinvt	involvement of users/comm. in service planning/consultation
	welfare	welfarism, dependency
Success measures	effective	evidence of effect
	impact	measure of health impact
	indicator	indicators of health
	measinform	information used in planning
	measures	information and success measures – general
	target	specified measurable target
Joint working	account	accountability/reporting responsibility for work
	haz	health action zones
	hfa2000	healthy city/HFA2000 work
	hon	Health of the Nation
	jointwork	joint working between departments and agencies
	politics	political control, democracy
	priority	health or service priorities
	relations	relationships between departments and agencies, culture
	strategy	health strategies and policies

Search strategy

Once coded, the data were searched using Ethnograph v4 to derive overall frequencies across all the codes and files. The cumulative line count and percentage of total is shown in Table 3. The total line count across all the transcripts was 31,550. Percentages do not add up to 100 because some sections are coded with multiple codes, while others remain uncoded. This confirmed impressions of main areas of interest in the discussions and directed the search strategy for text analysis. While coding strategies develop as main themes emerge, leading to less frequent use of codes that lie outside the main areas of discussion, this gives a broad indication of the main areas of concern in the discussion. Table 4 groups the codes in order to show this more clearly. Infrequently cited codes were generally not used for searching except where codes obviously are closely related to each other or to a main theme, for example welfare (0.3 per cent) and inequal (3.6 per cent).

Table 3. Cumulative lines for each code and percentage of total

Code word	Cumulative lines	Percentage total lines*
access	355	1.1
account	818	2.6
adults	6	0
budgets	1206	3.8
children	795	2.5
commaction	2903	9.2
commdevt	918	2.9
comminform	1215	3.6
commsaf	231	0.7
contracts	142	0.5
disabil	70	0.2
economy	426	1.4
econregen	707	2.5
education	1184	3.8
effective	305	1.0
environt	708	2.5
envtserv	1175	3.7
haz	145	0.5
healthiss	435	1.4
healthserv	1664	5.3
hfa2000	1673	5.3
hivaids	71	0.2
hon	532	1.7
housing	1924	6.1
impact	537	1.7
indicator	494	1.6
inequal	1141	3.6
leisserv	1569	5.0
lifestyles	434	1.4
measinform	659	2.1
measures	447	1.4
mentalill	78	0.3

Table 3. *continued*

Code word	Cumulative lines	Percentage total lines*
mentalprom	343	1.1
needasst	781	2.5
networks	463	1.5
nimby	456	1.4
oldpeople	97	0.3
parenting	199	0.6
physact	789	2.5
politics	1843	5.8
poverty	445	1.4
priority	257	0.8
pubhlth	1667	5.3
purchase	152	0.5
quallife	1360	4.3
relations	2445	7.7
safety	271	0.9
smoking	93	0.3
socserv	1678	5.3
strategy	2199	7.0
submis	125	0.4
target	64	0.2
tradstand	38	0.1
transport	179	0.6
userinvt	3865	12.3
welfare	104	0.3
resources	1197	3.8

* Percentages do not add up to 100 owing to multiple coding, and uncoded sections

Table 4. Rank order of codes by percentage of total lines

Codes	Percentage of total
1. userinvt	10+
2. commaction; relations; strategy; housing; jointwork: politics; socserv; pubhlth; hfa2000; healthserv; leisserv	5–10
3. quallife; resources; education; budgets; envtserv; comminform; inequal; commdevt; account; econregen; children; environt; needasst; physact; measinform	2–4.9
4. networks; impact; hon; indicators; poverty; nimby; measures; lifestyle; healthiss; economy; access; mentalprom; effective	1–1.9
5. adults; commsaf; contracts; disabil; discount; haz; hivaids; mentalill; oldpeople; priority; smoking; subsmis; target; tradstand; transport; welfare	< 1

Generally discussion focused on process issues of joint working and relationships, issues to do with working with the community and quality of life and less on specific health topics or target groups in the community. Where discussed these were usually presented as examples to illustrate a more general point. It was decided not to search on these issues, but to refer to examples of action as they appeared in other sections of the text. Depending on the size of the sample, searches were either conducted using single search codes, or multiple search codes, where this was mostly to subdivide responses into different service perspectives. In all, 57 searches were undertaken across the dataset (Table 5).

Table 5. Code word search strategy

Single searches	Multiple searches
inequal	userinvt +socserv
welfare	userinvt +education
poverty	userinvt +leisserv
quallife	userinvt +envtserv
	userinvt +housing
networks	userinvt +pubhlth
nimby	userinvt +healthserv
commdevt	
needsasst	commaction +socserv
comminform	commaction +education
	commaction +leisserv
impact	commaction +envtserv
effective	commaction +housing
measures	commaction +pubhlth
indicator	commaction +healthserv
measinform	
target	commaction +userinvt
hfa2000	jointwork +socserv
hon	jointwork +education
haz	jointwork +leisserv
	jointwork +envtserv
account	jointwork +housing
politics	jointwork +pubhlth
	jointwork +healthserv
strategy	
priorities	relations +socserv
	relations +education
resources	relations +envtserv
budgets	relations +housing
contracts	relations +pubhlth
purchase	relations +healthserv
economy	
econregen	

All searches were printed and reread in the thematic groupings listed in Table 5. Sub-themes and issues across the extracts were identified and quotations marked. Linkages and overlaps between areas were noted and the data are presented under the headings of the following broad themes:

- quality of life
- poverty, inequalities and economic regeneration
- working with the community
- joint working and relationships
- priorities and strategies
- HFA2000 and Health of the Nation
- political influence and accountability
- measuring success.

3. Quality of life

Improving the quality of life for local residents was clearly seen to be an important local authority role. There was a feeling that local authorities were in a unique position to influence quality of life and a positive sense of community, and that this was a key aspect of their function:

> 'The council generally accepts that its role is to be the focus of all services that are needed to support a community as a complex organism, and we see health as one of our principal partners . . . I think that [developing a sense of community] is very much important in its focal role, there is no other body that is statutorily placed in the position of representing the total community. That's the council's role.' (X1)

> 'If this sense of community improves health, let's assume it does, I don't see how the health service can engender that sense of community. The only organisations that could, I would have thought, are local authorities. I think it's a question of scale. People have a size they can relate to . . . a local authority is probably as big as they can relate to as far as what they would call community.' (E2)

Quality of life was perceived in both negative and positive ways, and council actions were apparent in both improving poor quality of life for the disadvantaged and providing opportunities for enhancing quality of life in the wider community.

These will be considered under the two headings below :

- improving poor quality of life
- positive enhancement of quality of life.

Improving poor quality of life

Poor quality of life through increased levels of stress, anxiety, depression, anti-social behaviour and social isolation was seen to be associated with ill health . From the housing perspective these were concerns that were frequently described:

> *'People living in tower blocks . . . do not know and are frightened of their neighbours. Crime and fear of crime, particularly amongst elderly people is creating a circle of tension and a circle of isolation . . . where people are frightened to go out and they have no community link . . .'* (H2)

> *' . . . quality of life is writ large as one of our guiding principles to protect and, if possible, enhance the quality of life . . . If our estates are nice places to live that also contributes to the wellbeing of our citizens . . . Perhaps more the mental than the physical wellbeing . . .'* (H1)

The contribution of mental wellbeing to physical health was recognised, although the relationship with health was not always direct. Community perceptions of problems in their housing or environment were more likely to be the presenting problems, the link through mental ill health to physical ill health was not always evident but was recognised:

> *'There are other things that are much more difficult to see as they relate to health. If there are things that upset people and make them feel stressed and depressed and you know that their area is being neglected . . . that's all mental health, and once you've had your general wellbeing lowered then you're more susceptible to the rest of it, germs and everything else that comes along.'* (E4)

One respondent who had discussed with his staff their contribution to health prior to the interview emphasised that dealing with isolation and loneliness was identified by 'people who are supposed to be improving housing' as 'absolutely crucial in how they perceive people's wellbeing and therefore potentially their health' (H2). However this contribution to health and wellbeing was not always felt to be valued by the health service:

> *'I think there might be perhaps a little more honesty on behalf of the medical side of health that they are not the ultimate total determinants of people's wellbeing in health, and that local authorities have a legitimacy in health issues. I don't think they really buy it at the moment . . . It's almost as if the work that we do in trying to improve the quality of our housing stock, improve its environment, reduce crime, deal with community safety, are secondary issues compared with the incidence of breast cancer or identifiable diseases.'* (H2)

In terms of improving the quality of life, housing departments clearly felt that this was a responsibility, not only for the tenants in their own housing stock, but for the wider community as well. In terms of housing allocations the council had a responsibility to ensure that it was shaping the community by introducing a mix of types of people and building networks. By so doing they would avoid overconcentrations of at-risk or socially excluded groups:

> *'If you have these communities how do you begin to cut across what makes them socially excluded? And that's where there are issues . . . you don't concentrate all your poorest, unemployed single mothers all in one block or estate because obviously it's much harder to deal with that as an issue than it is if you have a mixture of people.'* (H5)

However, the way in which this was done was not just about improving the bricks and mortar, but to do with the manner in which the council related to the community. These themes will be discussed in more depth in the sections on community and user involvement (Chapter 5) but they are touched upon here in the sense of the wider approaches to improving quality of life:

> *'Back to quality of life again, the council can't do anything . . . unless it joins successfully with the community itself, so the community's got to take it back as it were. Who's responsible for the quality of life on council estates? Ultimately the people who live there . . .'* (H1)

This role was seen to be a facilitating and empowering approach, and not, as the same respondent said, 'telling people how to live their lives, or making decisions in a paternalistic, patronising way, we know what's best . . . stop doing that . . . and start asking the community what it wants'.

Positive enhancement of quality of life

Those working in leisure departments viewed quality of life and the council's role in improving it in a more positive way. The main routes stated were through physical activity and positive use of leisure time through arts and recreation facilities, or simply maintaining the environment to be enjoyed by all sections of the community.

> *'I think if we are serious about people's quality of life in its widest sense and about making life better for as wide a group of people in the community as possible then leisure has to have a very important part.'* (L1)

Tourism had an interesting role to play in improving the quality of life for residents through improving the economy and the environment, although the health implications were less immediate:

'Our mission statement is to develop tourism within this district for the benefit of the economy whilst managing the development in such a way as to improve the quality of life for its residents. There is a balance [between] visitor, host community and environment.' (L4)

'Tourism . . . is all about a sense of place, a sense of ownership, belonging and pride . . .'
(L2)

Although a non-statutory function, tourism and development of the arts and culture through museums and art galleries were seen as important avenues, and there was recognition that different approaches were necessary for different parts of the community. Encouraging physical activity in more ways than just encouraging uptake of leisure facilities, organising tea dances, for example, was seen as a way of improving the quality of life for some. The contributions of leisure departments to promoting quality of life were many and varied:

'There's a growing recognition that, sort of, the wider wellbeing of people apart from just exercise is increasingly important and giving people something which is stimulating. So, you know, leisure in the city is arts and heritage, it's not just recreation, it's parks, it's conservation, it's environment . . . it's about quality of experience . . .' (L1)

'I think a lot of what we do is about mental health, frankly. The things which give people self-respect, self-fulfilment, give them a feeling of achievement and worth . . .' (L2)

'People get into problems, in difficulty and it affects their health as much as other aspects of their lives where they feel disconnected. The sorts of things that we do, should, if we are successful in doing what we do, help people to feel connected with place, the community and with each other and indeed with themselves. So that's what we are all about, it seems to me.' (L2)

4. Poverty and inequalities

Reducing poverty and inequalities were central concerns of local authority officers. Five groups of issues emerged in the discussions. These were:

- identification of ways in which local authorities could contribute to reducing health inequalities through their access and targeting services to disadvantaged groups in the community
- the particular problems of the recognition of rural inequalities
- difficulties and opportunities for partnerships with health authorities on joint work to reduce inequalities
- concerns about the negative effects of targeting disadvantaged groups in specified geographical patches
- economic regeneration.

Service access and provision to disadvantaged groups

Social services departments are in contact with young families and children, and housing departments with some of the poorer sections of the community through direct provision of housing and benefits advice services. There was an impression, however, that the opportunities for integrating services and maximising the potential of such contacts was not used to the full. For example, in housing and in social services:

> 'For council tenants, for example, how can it be that 75 per cent of our tenants are on benefit, but we concern ourselves with the technical nature of the quality of their dwelling alone? What is this nonsense? Huge technical function, wonderful rewiring of rooms and things, but where is the interface between poor people, in many cases in poor housing, and employment and training, where is it?' (H2)

'. . . nationally we have not as a profession addressed the health needs and looked after kids well enough . . . in the past . . . but I would want to be sure that we were making sure we had good health records for the kids we look after and made sure that they had all their immunisations . . . you've got a captive group of kids who are disadvantaged from when you have contact with them and that disadvantage will include knowledge about their own health . . . we should be spending time talking individually or in groups with those children.'

(S1)

Access to advice services was one way of recognising clients' immediate needs and then being able to address underlying health problems. Often this was through advice officers having information about support groups and services that they could pass on. Occasionally they became more actively involved in health issues through provision of displays and information in advice centres. Conversely it was noted that benefit advice provided from health premises, such as doctors' surgeries, could also be valuable, particularly for those not wishing to present with a financial problem, who 'feel safe in their doctor's surgery because there is an element of trust and confidence' (H4). It was also noted that it was easier to obtain time off work to visit the doctor than the benefits advice centre.

Difficulties in accessing disadvantaged groups, particularly with respect to needs assessment, were also noted. In housing, for example, articulate middle-class residents often get their voices heard over those of social housing residents who may be dispersed in scattered housing stock. The establishment in one authority of a 'cross-tenure group' facilitated by the council enabled them to get a clearer picture of the concerns of the social housing tenants, which were found to be similar to those of the private sector – traffic, crime and lack of children's facilities, for example (H6). A similar point was made by an education officer:

'. . . there tends to often be a middle-class takeover . . . and I think somehow the councils almost need to protect those groups from takeovers by interested parties.' (D2)

Conversely, the concern not to concentrate the socially excluded in one block or estate in order to avoid creating socially divided communities could also lead to difficulties in accessing the needy and hearing their voice.

Other opportunities to target services or increase uptake by disadvantaged groups included, for example, leisure services providing discount or incentive schemes for those on benefits, young people and students which cover access to leisure centres and other forms of recreation, such as art galleries; and environmental health provision of geothermal heating to council properties at a lower cost than gas or electricity, with the possibility of extension into poorer areas of privately owned properties.

Rural inequalities

The problems of rural inequalities and relative poverty were also noted, in that they exist in affluent areas, and it is sometimes more difficult to get colleagues to focus attention on these issues. There was a recognition of the way that more affluent communities hide their problems, and that revealing them could cause political difficulties:

'The community of —— does very well to hide its poorer communities and in fact the poorer elements . . . go shopping elsewhere . . . in cheaper communities so they also hide themselves.'

'The poverty isn't hidden to those people who know the area well . . . but there are some political agendas about what we are allowed to surface . . . and what it just wouldn't probably be politically acceptable to touch . . .' (S3)

There was evidence, however, that such local authorities were in a position to begin to take a strategic view on poverty, and that they recognised the need to 'pull that into the health arena as well' (X1).

Partnerships with health

Concerns were expressed about the apparent lack of interest in health inequalities from the health sector and the difficulties in maintaining links between services:

' . . . if they actually looked at the health inequalities in —— [they] ought to be passionate, but in all the systems, organisation, administration are dreadfully dull and it doesn't seem to be a passion for health – I don't understand it.' (H2)

'I was in discussions with someone from the health authority about using our geographical spread . . . to promote the take-up of certain health benefits in some of the ethnic minority communities . . . We could have assisted in that. It didn't work because of the . . . organisational difficulty, the individual moved on and the connections went apart again . . .' (H4)

Difficulties of working across boundaries were also seen within an LEA where those working in child protection and with children educated at home because of illness or being excluded from school weren't actively engaged in alliances or joint work:

' . . . *they don't see themselves as having that as a responsibility . . . or they do but they just haven't got the scope, the people, the time, the resources to do it.'*   (D3)

Solutions to dealing with the needs of the disaffected, especially school exclusions, would be improved by 'pooling knowledge as well as potentially pooling resources', and one authority was planning to meet with other agencies to consider this (D2). Similarly, the issue of health service involvement over homelessness and regeneration issues had been considered at a chief officers' meeting in one area (H5).

Negative effects of targeting disadvantaged groups

There were also concerns about the potential negative effects of targeting specific areas or sub-sections of the community with specific initiatives to redress inequalities. The way services are actually provided could enhance divisions within a community rather than aid the process of community empowerment. Experiences were cited of moneys going into specific areas yet at the end of the programme the level of community participation was significantly less than before (H4). To avoid this it was suggested that approaches should 'be seen as being in the ownership of the community as a whole' rather than agencies determining what was appropriate for whom.

Identifying areas for regeneration necessarily leaves out other areas where inequalities may be dispersed within the community, or simply not so extreme as those in the designated areas.

'If the social exclusion unit goes back down the path of area-based regeneration . . . and links needs to areas rather than to problems, then we will always have problems with an area like this. There are parts of the country . . . where it always looks worse.'   (H6)

This was seen to be a potential problem in the designation of primary care group (PCG) areas. In one case the most obvious boundaries would lead to a concentration in one PCG of all the social problems and inequalities (H5).

Targeting was also seen as problematic if it perpetuated notions of 'welfarism' and dependency:

'We've inherited here a hugely welfarist approach of identifying people who need services and then of course we provide those . . . this welfarism, to me anyway, is the biggest

problem. You know we're still dishing out to those that are perceived to need most without really being clear about what's effective . . .'   (S2)

'We've lived in a society that has actually developed dependency. Actually not valued participation and the capacity of the community to address their own problems . . .' (H4)

The short-term nature of many projects funded to address specific community needs caused problems. Not only did the resources disappear from the area after a few years, but the knowledge and expertise held by the workers were lost to the authority (H6). Targeting was seen to be effective, however, when it was done on a very small geographic scale with local projects, such as resource and advice centres, in 'a very specific area with specific needs' (H5).

Economic regeneration

Local authorities were in no doubt about the relationships between the health of the local economy and the health of residents. Improving the economy was seen as a key role for local authorities:

' . . . that's what they should be about, the health and welfare of local people, and that widens out to, of course, economics because of the correlation between low incomes and lesser health . . .'   (E2)

A sound economic infrastructure was seen as 'the means for paying for health' (E1) and economic regeneration was undertaken through various schemes, such as the Single Regeneration Budget (SRB) bids and lottery funding opportunities. There were some concerns that regeneration should be broader than simply economic development, should encompass a more holistic notion that embraced not only employment but education, training, improved services and 'some creation of a community' (H2). In this way, it was felt, the links between economic regeneration and health were more clearly made, whereas economic development alone could sometimes lead to developments that were not health-promoting. Examples included shopping developments that would take businesses out of town centres and increase car usage (S1).

SRB bids had provided opportunities for joint planning with health authorities and greater involvement in planning issues by the community. In one area a community planning event for an SRB was considered to be one of the most successful planning events the council had held, engaging with wide sections of the community (S1).

In more prosperous areas, where policy decisions had been made not to develop industry in order to maintain the quality of the environment, tourism was seen to be a key economic driver: '. . . tourism actually helps the city keep its healthy ambience . . . ' (L4). However, the direct relationships between the economy and health were perhaps less apparent in a prosperous area than in deprived areas, where it is a more 'recognised issue'.

5. Working with the community

This chapter covers a range of issues discussed about ways of working with the community, involving users in service planning and delivery, and approaches to community development. A large proportion of the interviews focused on these topics, which are considered under the following themes:

- community development approaches to service delivery and organisational issues about community development services
- reactive community engagement through the provision of information
- proactive community engagement, considering the varied processes used to engage with the community, such as community action groups, or forums; community networks and support mechanisms; and the involvement of users and the community in assessing needs and priorities, service planning and consultation
- issues to do with adequacy of community representation
- the potential for considering health issues
- the potential for building social capital.

Community development approaches

Discussions about community development indicated a lack of distinction between community development as an approach or philosophy and as a service department or council function. Arrangements for community development were varied and often unclear, although its value was highly rated. The authorities had different mechanisms for community development, and within authorities these were often diffused across departments, or separate from other community liaison or action services:

> '[Community development is] different to community action, which is, I think, to some extent bringing people together, but I think community development is about empowerment . . . about bringing people together and making more out of the resources that're available, especially about people . . .'
> (L1)

'. . . *community development is a function over which council departments have fought for quite a long time. Leisure services . . . [have] always argued that community development is [their] responsibility but leisure services is relatively small compared with [all the] employees of the local authority and community development ought to be all of our responsibilities.'*
(H2)

On relationships between a community action section and community development within a local authority:

'*We do work alongside community development, but they are literally doing exactly what it says, they are helping individual groups or whatever to run committees to look at issues or whatever. I mean what we're doing isn't any of that, we don't do any of that kind of development with individuals or groups. I'm really a facilitator that helps them to address issues, and community development . . . develop the groups so they can address the issues.'*
(X2)

There was a sense that over recent years community development services had all but disappeared, but, now that there was a recognition of their potential and policy endorsement, they were reappearing in different parts of the council. There was a sense of history repeating itself, and a recognition that younger staff did not have the experience of the potential role of community development:

'*I mean it's almost come full circle, hasn't it, from community development, and now we are going back to community development. I think there is still some potential there for it.'*
(H5)

'*You know, I remember community development teams, but I think most of the people that are in my division don't!'*
(E5)

Where it did occur community development work was not limited to any particular population or age groups, with examples of work with play schemes to projects with older people. The potential of community development approaches to tap into community resources was recognised, for example, leisure services were involved in training people in the community to become football or rugby coaches on a voluntary basis, and this was seen to have an influence on problems associated with disaffected youth:

'*But if only people realised the talent and capacity that is actually out there, that we should begin to unleash and use that, and then you can actually begin to address many of the problems that we face . . .'*
(H4)

Community development was also seen as being a way of helping the council to have a better understanding of cultural issues and local community concerns than the health service. The impression was that the local authority workers were more closely engaged with the community on a day-to-day basis, but, while it might be possible to 'get the GPs to play' (H2), the health authority was far too remote to relate to the community.

The inclusion of community development processes in all aspects of work was seen to be vital to develop self-help and self-esteem and the notion of a self-sustaining community. The fragmentation of community development processes was seen to be an obstacle to achieving this, and the success in pulling 'disparate elements to . . . work together in one sort of organisational approach' would become the 'necessary bedrock in which things like health . . . could best be delivered' (H4).

Reactive community engagement

The provision of advice and information to the public was seen as part both of the process of empowerment and of involving the community more in the decisions the council makes and the way it delivers services. There were some examples of ways of providing opportunities for the community to approach the council for advice, which might then lead to the officers referring the individual on to other services or dealing with issues raised. In this sense these were examples of reactive engagement with the community, where the council responded to the issues brought to them.

One mechanism for this is the use of neighbourhood offices providing a 'decentralised generic front-ended service' to provide a 'seamless front' to the council to make it more accessible to the public (H4). For young people drop-in services for advice provided 'up-front, shop front' (D2) access for support. Information provision was also seen in terms of a medical model of health education, and the potential of the contact between council services and the public was emphasised again:

> ' . . . the council have lots of opportunities to talk to people, not just the official community interface like community action, but we have lots of places where people come to us all the time, like housing offices, civic foyers . . . '　　　　　(X2)

From a social services perspective this was taken further to reflect the responsibility of services to provide information in a proactive manner:

> 'I think there is an enormous amount of ignorance about health within the community, although it is getting better, and we so often deal with people who are not articulate and cannot get information themselves, and we therefore have a duty to provide information

in a way that people can use and retain.' (S1)

'One of the things that I think we've learnt in social services is that people use us as signposts more than we ever thought, and so as a department we need to be very informed and aware of what makes for Healthy ——, what the projects are, where the advice is, where the information can be found and we've got to contribute to that much, much more than we ever have done.' (S3)

Proactive community engagement

Interviewees described a number of ways in which their councils were actively seeking greater involvement of the community in needs assessment and service planning. These included community action forums, local ward committees, advisory panels and the like. The degree of engagement varied from consultation on specific issues in public meetings to delegated budgets and local decision-making. In most cases these were generally set up on a small neighbourhood basis. Some were relatively new or still in the process of establishment and others brought together existing smaller groups under one umbrella. However, there were some exceptions, where mechanisms had been established on a much larger scale. Resources were required to support these schemes in the nature of co-ordination and facilitation through identified officers, either within service departments or as a corporate community action team, both to establish the networks and service them in unsocial hours, and to 'act as a bridge between the council and the community, representing points of view backwards and forwards' (X2).

In housing there were examples of resident and tenant bodies, ranging from consultancy forums to tenant management organisations managing the council's housing stock:

'We've got a kind of customer forum which comprises people from across the whole of the district who tell us what they think about the service in their particular area . . . and below that we have customer panels which are tenants' associations for various parts of the district.' (H3)

'And where we are slightly unusual as a council is that we have devolved management of our housing stock whilst retaining ownership of the stock. So we have in effect managing agents who manage the council's housing stock and they are employed by the council's tenants and that's the tenant management organisation . . . where it is unusual here is that it is borough-wide . . .' (H6)

Another authority was in the process of establishing an extensive committee structure at ward level both to understand the needs of local residents and to empower them to become involved in local decision-making across departmental boundaries, through the devolvement of budgets and financial responsibility:

> ' . . . setting up ward advisory boards, bringing in residents' groups and other sectors of communities . . . and over a period of twelve months beginning to develop ward plans . . . like an audit . . . ' (H4)

> ' . . . [these] will assist, I think . . . in getting a truer picture of need and provision and how it's perceived and also it's just responsiveness generally in order to inform our planning and priorities processes . . . ' (S2)

> ' . . . the ward sub-committees are beginning this process, they've all been given small budgets of £50,000 each to aid, or encourage if you like, the flourishing of ideas about what the needs of local communities are.' (H4)

Creating community forums to bring together existing community groups and to provide opportunities to engage with other citizens on service issues was also evident.

> '[Community action forums] are wider than community groups and residents' groups . . . it's the bringing together of a number of community groups that might exist . . . [that] were doing different things and we brought them together within their identified boundaries.' (S1)

Within environmental health, work on Agenda 21 and sustainability issues had led to the establishment of environmental consultation panels which have been active in issues like transportation, waste management and pollution (E5). The use of the community care network established with the Council of Community Service was another way of accessing a range of community views used by social services (S3). The role of parish councils was potentially important in rural areas in reaching out to influential people in the community, but was not uniformly used:

> 'When we do major changes in services . . . we go to the parish councils and ask them for the names and addresses of all the groups or institutes or organisations in that area . . . then we write to them and say can we come and address you about . . . It's on the basis that those that operate those groups are the community leaders as such and so they'll live in the area . . . ' (E2)

> 'The primary conduit for local consultation for the council as a whole is the parish council.' (H1)

And conversely:

> ' . . . *we know we don't consult with parish councillors about issues . . .*'   (S3)

Other methods for needs assessment included the establishment of substantial consultation panels with representative samples of the population:

> ' . . . *a community advisory panel. There are 1500 people from different sections of the community, statistically selected, to give views on council activities or other activities, you can consult them [by questionnaire] on whatever you like.*'   (E1)

In education the provision of community education services from after-school clubs to adult education and projects for older people were cited as ways of working through the community (D2). In schools the establishment of benchmarks enabled one authority to engage with the wider community by encouraging and monitoring parental involvement in school development and service provision:

> '*The benchmarks for health promotion established clear sorts of involvement that schools should have with parents, and in fact we've monitored those levels . . . like parents involved in writing policy or attending parents' evenings.*'   (D1)

Community representation

In discussing involving the community many comments were made about the difficulties of adequately representing the community and the problems that this poses:

> '*I have my doubts whether some of the kind of tenants' associations and customer forums and community associations are truly representative by age profile and background, but at least you do have, if you like, a feedback about what's going on.*'   (H3)

> ' . . . *that sort of public interface of the public meeting, sort of 7.30 on a Wednesday evening, doesn't necessarily gain you access to the full range of the community . . .*' (H4)

It was also recognised that it was often those who represented a particular interest group or issue that were more likely to be active than the ordinary citizen:

> '*we've [consulted the community] through community forums which . . . tend to be organisations of the voluntary sector . . . [there are] contradictions sometimes of where the council consults the voluntary sector to ask what its citizens want, when in fact the*

citizens that live locally may well have a totally different perspective on it . . . ' (H4)

From an education authority perspective, the first level of community engagement was seen as the community of schools and their staff, and ensuring that there were ways of involving them in decision-making was important to break a 'dependency culture' (D2).

Increasing the power of community groups in decision-making can lead to tensions with the elected members of the wards covered, who feel that their role as councillors is to act as the voice of the people. However, there was a reluctance from certain members because it was seen as a threat to their position as 'spokespersons from these estates' (H3).

It was felt that involving the wider community was more likely when there is a pressing local concern, for example:

'Tenants will only miss EastEnders *. . . and only come along to public meetings if there's a real reason which impacts on their life.'* (H3)

'A lot of the issues that they want to talk about relate to rats and rubbish and road traffic and noise, and those are the things that they really are enthusiastic about . . . that they associate more easily with because they affect them.' (E4)

There was frustration at not being able to move beyond what were perhaps seen as negative reasons for engagement, as when residents were objecting to planned changes, to a more positive sense of collaboration on healthcare issues:

'Why should I bother to give up two hours of my time to go along to a town centre forum? What's the point? They tend to only turn up when there's contentious issues and we seem to have generated a bit of a culture in this country that you only support when you are objecting . . . ' (E3)

' . . . so often they are effective when there is a particular issue around, and a lot of the issues can be nimby-typish issues or protective issues. I think there is a scope for making some more of the issues "give us issues", give us some information, give us ways in which we can help ourselves.' (S1)

Potential for considering health issues

These 'nimby-type' attitudes were thought to affect the ability of such groups to address health issues. Where there was a service-related issue, such as a hospital closure or proposed local provision of mental health services, there would probably be interested response. However, attempts to use such meetings to discuss less immediate or apparently relevant health issues often met with failure. The general impression gained was that opportunities afforded by the creation of networks of community groups were only rarely taken to consider health or health service issues:

> 'We had an open public meeting about care in the community . . . and there was a terrific chap . . . who talked about the perception of what it was like to be labelled as a disabled person . . . and about seven people came.'

> ' . . . the people, members of the public who take part in the forums and the committees aren't making the link for themselves, and I guess that it's fair to say we're not making the link for them either.'
>
> (X2)

Regarding the closure of a mental health centre:

> 'I mean, how do you make that really interesting to residents in ———? I mean, there is a real issue about . . . the language and how is it really going to effect people in terms of the service change . . . '
>
> (H5)

Given the considerable investment in mechanisms for community engagement demonstrated in the small sample of local authorities visited, there would seem to be excellent potential for building on these links to consider health issues. The diversity of approaches is probably to be expected given the diversity of communities, and the range of expectations from such processes. Thus it is probably not important which methods are chosen as long as they are appropriate for the area and services involved. Councils do not appear to need to have an explicit policy on community consultation for a variety of approaches to flourish. What is clear is that there is a need for resources to develop mechanisms and sustain them, and it would be wise of health authorities to consider ways in which they could share and build on these rather than duplicate them. There is clearly a lot to be learnt about how to engage the community and maintain their involvement, and the difficulties of attempting to address health issues that are not of immediate concern. Apart from the efficient use of service resources, combining health and local authority mechanisms makes sense for the individual too:

> 'The challenge for joint working would be . . . well, as a member of the community you don't want to go to three community forums, do you? One for health, one for social services and one for your local borough council. You want to go to one and see . . . information presented from the major agencies . . . '
>
> (S3)

Potential for building social capital

Apart from improving the direct links between community engagement and health issues, the current focus on environmental and social aspects has an impact on health itself. In addition, there will be a longer-term impact of delegation of power and decision-making to communities on individual and community empowerment, and potentially on the creation of social capital:

'*Not only are we getting empowerment, we're also getting volunteers, because the estate is theirs, not mine, so issues which are problematic on their estate can be resolved by the co-operation . . . of those individuals who live on the estate trying to police problems . . .*'
(H3)

' *. . . let's get a given sum of money and let's just simply take it to the community. Let them decide how to spend it, our job's to facilitate it and provide the professional expertise that goes into that. It's their street, let them decide whether they want – bollards or slow-down bumps or whatever . . .*'
(H1)

Discussions in one area with a local community project about opening up access to a land-locked area found that the residents:

' *. . . would have liked that back land to remain fairly wild, butterflies, slow worms and things like that. We said, well, that's OK, but we have a maintenance problem keeping it up and we have complaints from people in that locality, what are you going to do about it? The answer was, we'll look after it. You provide us with some labour over a weekend and invest in some kind of equipment . . . we'll do the rest and once we've got it up to scratch we'll take it on. And we've done that. They keep it on so we've actually reduced maintenance costs.*'
(H3)

Other examples of where community action had made real changes in communities were cited, and frequently these related to concerns with young people. Where there had been complaints about youth problems, these could be turned around by consulting with the young people and the local community to come to a locally owned solution, such as the creation of simple 'kick-about' areas or a skateboarding park:

'*So one of the main themes that seems to come through [from community forums] is catering for the needs of younger people. Provision of sports facilities but in consultation with the local young people . . . Kick-about areas, informal sorts of areas have been wanted by youngsters – basketball-type rings and that sort of thing. They've been actually installed in places where young people want them, where they don't cause*

nuisance as well to the nearby, perhaps elderly, residents.' (E1)
' . . . *the police got involved, they were called out regularly, damage was being caused to an extent to the car park. We provided the facility down —— Park and it's been like a magnet, it's taken all the young people away from the sensitive areas down to a facility where they can use it without causing anybody any trouble and . . . do their own thing. In a way that's all they ever wanted.'* (L1)

The role of the council in supporting and enabling community groups to flourish was seen as a hands-off one:

'So in terms of our role, it is very much trying to provide logical linkages between very effective delivery points on the ground to see whether we can (a) help them, (b) provide appropriate co-ordination where it is necessary and (c) fill the gaps . . . ' (D2)

Throughout there was a recognition that these changes in relationship between the council and the community took a long time to establish and would evolve over time:

' . . . *you've got to keep flogging away at it . . . you've got to keep going at it and you've got to demonstrate bit by bit. It's an incremental process. You won't do it in five minutes, you might do it in five years, but that's the type of timescale you would take to get to a point of true meaningful community empowerment.'* (H1)

6. Joint working and relationships

Interviewees were asked about current ways in which they worked jointly with the health service, and between local authority departments. The problems and difficulties of joint working were often described as being structural and organisational rather than relating to individuals, however, some positive examples and opportunities for further joint work were cited. These comments are considered under the following headings:

- structural and organisational constraints
- differing perceptions of health
- interdepartmental joint work
- joint work with primary care
- successes and opportunities.

Structural and organisational constraints

The upheaval caused by NHS reorganisations was frequently mentioned as having had an adverse effect on relations and joint work between health and local authorities:

> 'What's happened over the last five years is that those five authorities have become one . . . with this provider purchaser split and the formation of the NHS trusts, they became much more inward-looking . . .' (E4)

> 'the health authority [has] been driven by performance measures and waiting lists and all the rest of it and they've been busy justifying what they've been doing . . .' (E3)

'The problem with the health authority is quite frankly that the pieces have been moving on the board every – it seems like every week, but it's about every year. Now that we've got the settled pattern, what we are addressing throughout the county is how we consult . . . There are a number of areas where we haven't really built up the contacts and I think it's partly because people have been so busy restructuring health, and people's desks have been moving.'
(X1)

Differences between health authorities in their working processes can cause difficulties for local authorities working across a number of health authorities. Differences in target-setting, priorities and funding arrangements can create different models of working which a single agency has to adapt to while attempting to deliver an equitable service across a county (D3). These could be overcome more easily where there was clarity in management arrangements:

'When I look at the other two health authorities I know instantly whose responsibility it is for that sort of liaison and so on, and it doesn't work like that in the other health authority. I guess it reflects the value perhaps that they place on the work . . . '
(D3)

Conversely, where local authority boundaries were smaller than the health authority, 'the loyalty of an NHS management team is always going to be to a wider area', leading to 'a degree of insensitivity to local requirements, local needs' (E5).

The sheer scale and complexity of joint working was frequently cited as overwhelming good intentions. Criticisms were made of the 'lack of clarity of purpose and intention' in health in comparison to education (D2) and the plethora of groups engaged in planning. For example, in relation to child and adolescent mental health:

'There are a massive number of groups, and I keep sending people to groups and then find there is another group and say to the health authority we cannot afford all these, let's just have one group that looks at these particular strategic intentions.'
(D2)

' . . . now there's a lot of concern . . . as to how we could be represented on those groups because there is no slack in anyone's organisation these days. There are not the personnel to do all this as well as people might want to do it.'
(D3)

The loss of control and power was indicated as being another barrier to more joint work:

'Sharing resources we could do double the work . . . but everybody's hanging on to what they've got because they're frightened if they let a little bit go they'll be seen as non-important . . . if you go and share resources with somebody else you must make sure that this project's big and everyone notices how good it is.'
(L3)

Education services mentioned the difficulty of health authority misunderstandings about the availability of their resources for joint actions. Often they could not afford to take desirable actions because over 90 per cent of budgets is devolved to schools (D3). Where relationships between individuals in health and local authorities were very good, cutting through the bureaucracy was often dependent on the trust built up:

> '. . . because in one area where the working together is very good you can talk about total health and . . . the fragile nature of budgets, and you can talk about developments . . . because you put your budgets on the line and you know they won't be abused and get taken for granted.' (S3)

This was more likely to be evident where there had been tangible joint action:

> '. . . what I managed to get was some of that area's sport and leisure officers going to talk to the commissioning teams . . . I think it's perhaps through individuals knowing that [linkages] exist rather than there being a structure that they can fit into . . .'

However, there were sceptical views expressed about the practicalities and benefits of joint working with health:

> 'I'm trying to rack my brains how you would perhaps align health and tourism. I don't think you can . . . I think it's just a case of having the contacts and the network and people you know that you can contact as you develop a new aspect of what is going on. Perhaps that's the answer, if the communication lines are there, if necessary they can be activated.' (L4)

> 'I've more or less given up on alliances really, but . . . obviously . . . I'm going to have to do it somehow. But my heart sinks actually because I feel there's a great risk of investing a huge amount of time and effort for quite little reward . . . I don't think the alliance at the moment is that much more than a means of information exchange . . . I can't give you an example of a project or a policy that I've changed as a result of health authority representation and that's a bit dismal, isn't it really?' (E5)

Differing perceptions of health

Other constraints were less structural and more to do with the differing perceptions of health relating to 'different professional outlooks. None is better or worse – it's just different' (H1). From the local authority perspective health was repeatedly seen as being more to do with social and environmental determinants, and about mental as well as physical wellbeing. These differences in outlook proved to be a major obstacle in joint working. For example, the public health function in health authorities was considered to have been skewed towards treatment issues:

> *'It [the public health function] should span the two organisations in that I think there is a real danger in the current system because the NHS is about treatment primarily so the public health focus is often about, well, reducing treatment levels, which is a very different focus to the far more generic public health focus that you get at the community level . . .'* (D1)

Health service priorities and strategies were felt to relate more to physical health and specifically treatment rather than service integration and prevention:

> *'Well, I can't get away from thinking that the health authority priority is dealing with people when they become ill, and anything else is second to that, whereas our priority would be dealing with preventing people from becoming ill in the first place . . . '* (E2)

> *' . . . I look at an awful lot of strategies and my comments are always the same . . . This has been written from a health perspective . . . from a treatment perspective, it's the same in every group we go to and it misses so many opportunities . . . '* (D1)

Interdepartmental joint work

Interdepartmental working was frequently mentioned as being easier to execute than work between health and local authorities, often because the client base and their needs were seen as more similar. For example between housing and health versus social services:

> *' . . . we're dealing with 6000 people, and if you look at a population of 100,000, it's minute, right? They have bigger fish to fry. In the past I've always felt that you might get some crumbs from the table if we've dealt with health, and perhaps I'm instrumental in our difficulties, because it almost seems to me to be too much effort to, kind of, involve them at the end of the day. They are willing listeners . . . [but] we have to sell ourselves far greater with little reward . . . in terms of my time resource it's not worth the effort. I get a fair hearing from social services, I think that's back to the client . . . one can actually see that we're helping these people.'*

> *' . . . they are our clients and they are their clients and therefore the interrelationship is inevitable.'* (H3)

In another authority the joint work between housing and social services was facilitated by a combined housing and social service strategic function. The clearer focus given to joint issues through this was thought to have possibly strengthened links with health (H6).

Within and between authorities there were examples cited of difficulties arising at a senior level between departments but good co-operation at lower levels and vice versa. Whilst not indicating any clear pattern, it suggests that assumptions should not be made about the degree of co-operation existing at other levels in and between organisations from a particular perspective:

> 'This authority is very vertically structured . . . you get . . . powerful department(s) who operate in the vertical interest of that department. You go down to the bottom level . . . and relationships across are excellent . . . the field workers labour under the same difficulties, and so long as they are enabled to come into contact with each other . . . then they will work collaboratively. The problem is trying to make sure their collaborative working continues as you work up an organisation and attitudes become more selfish . . .'
> (H2)

> ' . . . although we have an alliance at a very senior level . . . I don't see an alliance mentality penetrating much below that senior level.'
> (E5)

Bringing services together in new unitary authorities was seen to be an advantage to promote better interdepartmental working on health:

> ' . . . we now have control over some of the health-related services. Social services is obviously one, the youth services another one and education is certainly another aspect . . . for many years we've moved around and touched on health issues but really felt it was quite difficult for us to take a lead and I think that is less of a case now.'
> (L1)

Yet achieving practical co-ordination of services within an authority was not always straightforward. The suggestion in one area of rationalising the workload of social workers and education welfare officers to avoid duplication of services to families 'sent shock waves' (D2), and led to a joint meeting of education, social services and health to consider the needs of the socially excluded.

Joint work with primary care

There were relatively few examples of areas where GPs and primary care teams were working with local authority staff on joint projects. Exercise referral schemes between

GPs and leisure services were one obvious example of a structured approach (L2). The potential for closer involvement was recognised, for example, social workers might benefit from 'being sited in primary care centres' (S2) to help with the management of social and health care for people entering hospital (S3). From an education viewpoint:

' . . . more and more now the GP is leading a team of other professionals, all of which have a major impact on primary health care, and a lot of which actually have more time to have an impact within the community and working with the school.' (D1)

However, for the most part respondents had little contact with GPs, or had had difficulties in trying to engage their interest. It was felt that this was due to their status as self-employed contractors and the pressures of their work. From an environmental health perspective:

'I've just not been able to access the GP world. We have tried to do it again and again by writing to GPs, trying to solicit interest. People are running asthma clinics and so forth but we've never, ever been able to generate anything substantial at all.' (E5)

Respondents were not optimistic about the ability of the planned primary care groups to achieve greater gains in partnership work, and there were concerns that primary care group development work was taking place without consultation with the local authority:

' . . . we are heavily involved [with the development of the primary care group] in —— but I know that there are some areas where consultation with social services hasn't taken place.' (S3)

Successes and opportunities

Various successful projects were mentioned that had been organised by a local health alliance, or had come out of specific aspects of service work. The following are examples that were given in the course of discussion and are provided as illustrations of the types of joint activity under way. Contributions of environmental health included air quality monitoring for an asthma alliance; homecheck services for accident prevention in children and the elderly; work on low-income nutrition and workplace health promotion. With housing and health there were projects on homelessness, for example. In these cases the authority had broadened out from the specific task to an acknowledgement of its wider impact on health, for example:

'It's not a statutory duty to go out and resolve the noise complaint because of the stress

it caused . . . what you can do is to use the noise powers that you've got . . . to start chipping away at that problem in conjunction with the police and the housing people . . . and you just need to keep sight of that bigger picture instead of . . . another job done, get rid of it.' (E3)

A number of opportunities to increase links between health and education were referred to, such as bringing together the health promotion services of both health and local authorities into one organisation. One example of complex joint funding arrangements between a number of health authorities and education authorities made possible the support of a team of skilled education advisers for personal, social and health education. The partnership arrangements also enabled the health authorities to have 'a voice in policy-making, policy decisions and the production of guidelines for schools' (D3). In another area education challenged the right of the health authority to have automatic access to children in schools in a 'bulk delivery environment' which was in the HA's interest in terms of cost-efficiency. Out of this came an agreement on each school's core entitlement to health services plus optional extra health education of the school's choice that would in effect be 'payment for the right to enter our premises' (D2).

One problem frequently mentioned was the lack of clarity of referral routes between agencies, so the development of a jointly resourced service model with relevant staff based together was suggested. Creation of a first-time parenting service would 'make better sense of the work of health visitors, practice nurses . . . and pre-school workers' (D1). The possibility of closer partnerships between health and leisure in the Healthy Living Centres initiative was welcomed, although at the time of the interviews it was not clear what form this might take.

Despite the criticisms and difficulties there was still a great deal of optimism:

'I think all those areas . . . have the potential for local government to work very closely with a lot of other agencies, including some people in the health field in the future. I don't think we've really done that in the past in all honesty, I don't think either side has got its act together in those terms, but I think there's a tremendous potential and . . . an awful wealth of momentum building up . . .' (L1)

' . . . it is a time for people being quite brave and taking the advantage that the White Paper, the Green Paper and the White Paper for Social Services . . . is going to pose us all with opportunities to change things and there are one or two people around who are really quite prepared to go out and say we can make a real difference here . . .' (S3)

The importance of trust in relationships and expectation of reciprocity of actions was stressed:

'. . . and so it doesn't matter that asthma is not on my agenda, it's about signing up to a common agenda and the next item I'm sure will be much more pertinent to [my] tasks and responsibilities . . .'
(S3)

Finally the key to success seemed to be honesty and realism in relationships between different partners:

'But let's just identify, be honest and realistic about it and say yes, I can help you do that, I am interested in that, but I'm not interested in that because I'm off in another direction . . . We can all buy into the sort of motherhood statement about what all these public bodies are interested in doing is improving the quality of life, but, you get back to work Monday morning, I get back to work Monday morning and we're all heading in different directions, so let's just be disciplined about what the area is and let's work to that.' (L2)

7. Developing joint health strategies

While there is inevitably some overlap between this chapter and some of the other themes, this attempts to focus on the planning, resourcing and contracting aspects of the organisations, the ways in which they could be brought together to address health issues, and the barriers to achieving that. The area will be considered under two main headings:

- determining joint priorities and strategies
- contracts, purchasing and resources.

Determining joint priorities and strategies

Priorities and strategies relating to individual departmental strategies, and single organisational strategies drawing together the priorities of different sections within an organisation, were described. However, work towards joint health strategies between local authorities and the health service and other partners was generally embryonic, but there was clear indication that this was accepted as the way forward. While joint planning mechanisms allowed health, social services and the key voluntary agencies to work together at a strategic level 'it doesn't work in terms of embracing community health' (S3). There was a need to understand the different emphases of different organisations but to work together in the 'areas of overlap' (L2). 'Greater clarity' was needed 'to fill the strategic gap' in order to understand the potential contributions from all the agencies, the 'commonalities' in order to determine 'priorities across all the elements', but realism is essential:

'Be clearer about what we are out to achieve and from the outset be realistic about what

we can achieve, given that resources are so scarce . . .'　　　　　　　　(H1)

The problems of drawing together joint strategies were recognised but there was a feeling of needing a pragmatic approach and thinking beyond professional boundaries to move things forward:

> *'The secret in really being effective is clearly to look at it from a strategic point of view and try to look at . . . actually what we are trying to achieve at the end of the day . . . and are there things in this service [that are] actually contradictory to objectives in another service and if they are how can we get round that and get some sort of sense into it. So coming at it from the centre as opposed from the service is, I think, the right way round.'*　　　　　　　　(L1)

Finding the right starting point was an issue, whether strategies should be top-down, directed from central government, or bottom-up, but:

> *'If you are going to do it from the ground-up basis, it's altogether more difficult, more time-consuming and less easy to define . . . the areas of overlapping interest and the overlapping objectives.'*　　　　　　　　(L2)

The need for a 'champion' to drive the process was important:

> *' . . . you've got to have the commitment to push it through and I think sometimes you've got to bang a few heads against the wall and say you* will *take this on board as a priority.'*　　　　　　　　(E3)

This sense of moving from 'strategic visions' to focus on practical implementable plans was necessary to forge joint working:

> *' . . . sometimes you have to force people to sit down and talk to one another, so . . . particularly from the health authority point of view, we have got to develop a plan that says once you've established what the problem is what are we going to do about it?'* (E3)

Limitations of the process of agreeing joint strategies included lack of certainty about central policy directives, lack of good data and shared information about health:

> *' . . . there's been a huge state of flux by not knowing perhaps what clear priorities there are. There is a lot of structural uncertainty at the moment . . .'*　　　　　　　　(S2)

> *' . . . you've got to have some health data and facts to back up that decision-making process and my perception is that at the moment that particular process isn't terribly good*

*. . . It's more about individual priorities . . . about their own particular push [priority]
. . .'*
(E3)

Also there seemed to be a willingness to set their own house in order by determining interdepartmental organisational strategies first, and then testing these with the health authority. Conversely the health authority would produce their health strategy and then consult on it. There seemed to be a chicken-and-egg problem. Given the scale of the task, it seems not unreasonable to co-ordinate internal strategy first before going wider, but this obviously limited the scope of the strategy by reducing options at the outset and doesn't give out the clearest signals of the intention to work jointly. Contrast the two examples below of a 'health-owned' health strategy and a 'local authority-owned' health strategy, with the description given of the process used to derive a more 'community-owned' environmental strategy:

'. . . the strategy is fundamentally about what a health service is going to look like, what major questions do we have to be asking in order to know we're on the right course. It's a big consultation document . . . although we've seen the sort of pre-launch document and made comments, suggestions and amendments. But [it's] very much not focused on public health, it's focused on hospitals . . .'
(S2)

'. . . we are developing as a new authority the whole issue of the strategic assignment . . . members will shortly be receiving . . . a very large document laying out what are our current actions in relation to our health, where we would hope to be in five and twenty-five years' time . . . once we have determined what those strategies are then we will put them on the agenda for the meeting of the health authority and raise them with the trusts and other providers.'
(S1)

'We have an environmental strategy which we co-ordinate on behalf of the council which relates to the Local Agenda 21 process . . . we have quite a novel environmental forum sub-committee [consisting] of elected members . . . business sector and some commercial interests . . .'

Meetings held every few months are open to the public and they hold small group discussions which are used to identify what needs to be addressed (E4).

Developing the strategy, however, should not be seen to be an end in itself:

'The trouble is by the time it's been hauled through so many consultative mechanisms that you forget . . . where you started. I think it is something you do just check from time to time that you are in line with . . .'
(D2)

The political influence is often the constraining factor in the way the process is developed, with members having to have a lead role in determining priorities before formal consultation with other agencies.

> *'Which isn't to say we haven't shared with colleagues in health, particularly in the Healthy City group . . . so there has been no attempt at secrecy . . . [but] you can't write at officer level the priorities of this authority.'*
> (S1)

Contracts, purchasing and resources

There were few positive examples of local authorities using contracts with their providers to influence health. One example was in leisure centre contracts requiring that anyone teaching exercise or physical activity is appropriately qualified (L3). There was a view that health service provider contracts were in 'an awful mess'. This was noted where health provider services had a direct impact on local authority services, such as two trusts which were providing different levels of school health services. Here the local authority was trying to use its influence to provide consistency and quality of service across schools in the area (D2). The same respondent also felt that 'health authorities and therefore public health within them have got so obsessed with managing the contracts . . . that they've lost the plot' with regard to public health (D2). Similarly another felt that there was 'a whole sort of mythology around purchasing' which was considered to be 'a bit of a distraction, because *[it]* is only a mechanism to get the services' (S2).

There seemed to be some confusion around the development of Health Improvement Programmes and what their ultimate content and purpose would be:

> *'Everyone's still lurching around, trying to figure out what it's really about, what it's going to involve . . . should it be healthy alliances or should it be a purchasing plan? . . . My own feeling is that it must be more like the healthy alliances strategy than a purchasing plan.'*
> (H5)

On funding issues there was repetition of the conflict between statutory and discretionary functions, and between loyalties to professional groups and to joint work:

> *'I think so many people are trying to fight their own particular corner to get limited resources to actually push for their own professional areas. Signing up to particular corporate things that could be a drain on those limited resources is a conflict which I think individuals have to make a decision about.'*
> (E3)

There was little evidence of current collaboration on joint resourcing, except on specific, usually time-limited, projects and posts. But there were many mentions of the need to pool resources in order to deliver on the health agenda. When pooling resources it was felt to be important to be explicit about constraints on funding and to share the responsibility for scarcity of resources, and not just to try and 'pass it on'. This necessitated talking openly about how resources were rationed:

> ' . . . to be successful in creating a true strategy [requires] talking openly about the need to ration.'
> (H1)

There clearly was not enough joint management of resources at the moment and this was felt to be a prerequisite for true joint work:

> ' . . . for alliances to be alliances, I think there needs to be, for a start, formal structures in which resources can be allocated and managed jointly.'
> (E5)

8. Health for All 2000 and Health of the Nation

This chapter looks at the influence of the philosophy and initiatives arising from the Health for All by the Year 2000 movement and the Health of the Nation strategy. In addition to the more general discussions on joint working these areas were specifically prompted to look at past and current alliance structures, the way in which Health of the Nation affected health alliance work and the interviewees' aspirations for change with the Green Paper *Our healthier nation*. These issues are addressed under the following headings:

- the involvement of individuals and departments in health alliances
- tensions in health alliances between strategic and project work, and the links between HFA and other initiatives, such as sustainability, Agenda 21 and community action
- the influence of Health of the Nation
- supportive mechanisms and opportunities.

Involvement in health alliances

Each of the local authorities had either current or past experience of HFA or Healthy City alliances. Respondents in one that had lost a structure for health alliance work keenly felt the gap that had been left. The alliance had 'stimulated thinking and activity in various departments' (E4) and had managed to get health implications as a requirement on all the council's committee reports. Although people still worked together a lot 'it's nowhere near . . . as proactive as it was' (L3) and 'the loss . . . means that there isn't any focus on health within the local authority and . . . it's extremely fragmented' (H2). In the other authorities there were many comments about the benefits of an alliance structure, although many recognised that it was a developmental process and had its limitations:

> '*I think what we have at best is an opportunistic programme where insofar as there are alliances they are actually between different council departments . . . I wouldn't sneer at those kind of internal alliances because it shouldn't be seen that the local authority is a sort of homogeneous entity at all . . . I think it's a good thing that the healthy alliances programme has encouraged this.*' (E5)

> '*. . . we're beginning to understand that health promotion or HFA actually affects every single aspect of our department, its technical services, its environmental health, its everything.*' (S3)

However, the role of health alliances was not always relevant to the everyday work of departments, and involvement of some individuals was occasional and dependent on the appropriateness of the topic under consideration:

> '*In terms of individual chief officers and how participative they are in the process I think it will depend on the particular agenda . . . it's the old story of what's in it for me? . . . To be honest I think they probably see it as a separate project. What they will do is use it as part of their toolbag of things they can dip into when it suits their particular agenda.*' (E3)

Representation of a department by an individual would not necessarily mean that all sections of that department were fully engaged. Thus in one education authority, although there was extensive involvement in a large number of district council HFA committees across the county by teacher advisers, the child protection section 'don't see themselves as necessarily having that as a responsibility' (D3) despite the obvious links with vulnerable children. The representation from health was also often limited to the public health section of the health authority, leading to it being a 'council and then health promotion initiative' with no representation from primary care or NHS trusts (H5).

Tensions and links between strategic and project work

Elsewhere we have seen the continuing dilemma for local authority staff in being involved in 'visionary' strategic work versus a well-defined tendency to prefer pragmatic activities with tangible results. This was equally true when the specific role of health alliance work was considered and was related to the stage of development of the alliance:

> '*When you try to get HFA embedded into an organisation you've got to get some quick*

successes because people have to see why we're bothering to do this . . . ' (E3)

Once an alliance becomes more established there is the need to balance the work of visible projects and the development of a more strategic role, which can lead to staff becoming 'torn between the strategic role and the project-based role' (E3). In this particular authority the alliance was just at the point of recognising and gaining approval for the development of a health strategy. The need to continue to have tangible projects is essential to maintain the pragmatic involvement of those with resource constraints:

> *'Give me a project which has a HFA label on it which needs our input and our resources . . . and we'll be right there. But . . . I've got to build a fence around the housing service, we can only do what we can do and it's actually better for us to concentrate on the pragmatic . . . '* (H1)

Links between strategy development in related areas were not generally well made. Whilst there was recognition of the overlap, with sustainability, for example, these policy consultations were often conducted separately (E1). Links between Agenda 21, HFA and anti-poverty strategies were also only just emerging in some areas:

> *'That pulling together of all the issues has not yet happened and that's probably because we didn't start with the strategic level . . . We are exploring how best to do it and from that we hope to put the mechanism in place . . . It may be that it is worth taking an extra few months' lead time to get it right.'* (X1)

There was also little evidence of good links between the health alliance and community action or community development work. In one authority where both avenues were well developed, involvement when it occurred was reactive only (X2).

Influence of Health of the Nation

The emphasis on lifestyle and targets in the Health of the Nation was thought to have skewed HFA work into more limited areas of individual behaviour rather than social health:

> *'We would argue that the HoN targets were health-driven targets and that they perhaps to an extent have distorted local planning, and we are attempting to redress the balance and say yes these are very important but here's some of our targets, the views that we representing the community want to have considered . . . '* (S1)

Health of the Nation was considered to have been 'made for the health authority with co-operation from the local authority' and that the local authority was not ever 'given a great deal of recognition in what we actually did do' (L3). The emphasis on individual behaviour put off some officers from becoming more involved:

> '. . . my concern is that if we're talking about HoN it's always about people's choice. My big concern is that it must never be the "thought police" which make people go down a certain path, we should make choices . . .' (L4)

Another found it difficult to communicate how, for example, schools were playing a part in reducing the targets when their educational actions were far removed from the direct health impact measured by mortality data (D3). However, the inclusion of the school as a focus in the Green Paper *Our healthier nation* was warmly welcomed, but:

> 'What's not welcome is if there are assumptions that schools will do things and are expected to do things that are unrealistic, for which they don't have the resources, the time or the support.' (D3)

However, the Green Paper was still disappointingly felt to be written as a health authority document and the targets, particularly the suicide target, were not considered relevant to the joint work on mental health that they had been involved in (H5).

Supportive mechanisms and opportunities

Repeatedly, the need for health alliance work to be part of the statutory functions of the local authority was mentioned, and for this reason HFA was always going to be vulnerable to budget cuts:

> '. . . it needs a higher profile. Councils of course are more easily able to cut money on discretionary duties than statutory ones, and HFA is a discretionary one so it doesn't get the same priority . . . If local councils had a duty to report on the health of the local population that would help because HFA would be one of the vehicles where that could be done.' (E2)

The role of the HFA co-ordinators was seen to be vital 'because they are trying to be a bridge between a number of organisations', and they needed more recognition and support because 'they are tactically working their socks off to bring people together at different levels' (S3). While initiatives like the Health Action Zones were welcomed, the expectation that they would bring about 'some wonderful synergy that's going to produce all kinds of exciting new things' was considered naive (H2). There was a very clear understanding that developing alliances took time and considerable effort, and the experience of many was that it brought considerable benefits, but much remained to be done.

9. Political influence and accountability

Political influence and accountability issues exerted considerable restraints on the ability of local authorities to address health issues and work jointly across departments and agencies, and interviewees noted many areas of tensions both within their own service delivery and their abilities to work with health services. These are considered under three main themes:

- the effects of different levels of governance
- constraints on joint work
- relationships between elected members and communities.

Effects of different levels of governance

The role of central government in determining priorities through the political system was clearly recognised, and the emphasis on statutory duties was a constraining influence on councils' activities in that resources were frequently stretched to meet statutory functions before discretionary joint work. Conversely there were those in the leisure sector who would welcome more statutory obligations as currently 95 per cent of leisure activity is discretionary (L1). The role of central government in modelling collective action between departments was seen as an important influence on the way local authorities work (S3). Where local MPs worked closely with the council, it was seen to strengthen community links and partnership with central government (E4).

In areas where there were county and district local authorities this created complexities in joint working in terms of levels of accountability and relationships with councillors. For example, over joint initiatives with social services:

' . . . I wouldn't dream of taking that to say Children and Families or the Social Services committee because it's not serious enough business, but for . . . [district council] . . . it's very serious.'

' . . . it's a stark realisation, isn't it, about how our structures are so very, very different. Sometimes we have city councillors who are also county councillors . . . and it's very difficult to know sometimes which hat they are wearing, how you lobby them and how you are mindful of the other hat . . .' (S3)

At this county level there was admission of the lack of consideration in involving the local democracy of parish councillors, and yet, as we have seen above, district council departments feel that they frequently work through them to engage the community. Conversely, in the unitary authority there was enthusiasm for the way in which the council was now able to work closely with previously county-level services to harmonise actions:

'So we are able to take a much rounder view than perhaps we were in the past when we were very limited in what we could do, we couldn't impinge, we couldn't force people working in social services to do things and to take actions that were in line with our policy because the political control of the county council has always differed from the political control of the city . . .' (S1)

Constraints on joint work

The differences between the democratic base of local authorities and the lack of accountability in health authorities was a recurrent theme that had an impact upon joint work:

'You see the health authority can, if you like, do what it likes in a way we can't, you know. We're driven by other pressures. I think this came out again and again in some of the arguments that took place in the development of the most recent health strategy for the area. There were issues about which the health authority, I think, were very frustrated . . .' (E5)

The lack of a democratic base, heightened by the lack of authority local representation on health authority boards resulted in health authorities being viewed as 'a highly centralised sort of quango-driven service' (H4). Community health councils were not perceived as being accountable to the community (E1) and thereby not filling this democratic deficit. Ironically the removal of local authority representatives from health authorities was also seen as having instigated more consideration of health matters:

'In the past we believed we were doing it because we had the right to nominate people to health authorities and, therefore, by nominating somebody to sit there you discharged the obligation . . . Now we no longer have that statutory linkage that's formalised, we have actually got to address what is our role with principal providers . . . in prevention services.' (X1)

Clearer joint accountability to the community through a public sector equivalent of a shareholders' annual general meeting was suggested, where achievements across agencies would be cited publicly, since 'the tax payers are our shareholders' (S3).

Political control also leads to restrictions on what issues local authorities can become involved in or 'allowed to surface' and 'what it just wouldn't . . . be politically acceptable to touch' (S3). The prerequisite for members to endorse joint actions led to tensions between partners, the chicken-and-egg problem, discussed in Chapter 7, of agreeing strategy with partners before seeking members' approval or vice versa, both likely to cause difficulties:

' . . . the anxiety has been that we develop a joint shopping list as officers and then the members get 25 of those shopping lists . . . and then not unsurprisingly say we can't do all these things, so we're not happy if you started hares running saying this is a commitment of the local authority which will have resource implications, before politically the members have decided on their priorities.' (S1)

Members' attitudes to their authorities being involved in health issues are also important – if they see health as being the sole prerogative of the health service they are unlikely to endorse actions to look at environmental impacts on health, for example (E5). There was a feeling that some members needed to increase their understanding of the potential benefits of joint working on health and that perhaps the agencies should share good practice with councillors. The inclusion of statements about health implications at the bottom of committee reports was one way of raising the profile of health issues with members (L3).

The nature of councils is not uniform. While some clearly adopted council-wide strategy development across departments and with other agencies, in another these did not explicitly exist, with obvious implications for health strategy development:

' . . . they will say we are a pragmatic council and pragmatic really means reactive rather than proactive . . . So you have implicit policies and you know when you've bumped into one that isn't acceptable . . . !' (D2)

'I think they don't like, as it were, highfaluting, idealistic kind of statements of . . . where

they are going . . . Now instead of having some grandiose theory . . . I think the politicians would say, well, make it nice, make it work . . . So instead of having a theory you do it in practice and see if people like it.'
(E5)

Concerns about re-election also impeded joint action, where councillors favoured actions that would result in short-term rather than long-term changes:

'Members being members want a bit of a quick fix because they obviously want to get re-elected and they want things so they can say: because of what I did this was the result.'
(E3)

Relationships between elected members and communities

In an area where councillors had pursued community involvement and delegated services to local level with electoral success this was seen by the officers to be driving their practice:

'The philosophy which the officers have to follow is a lot different to what it used to be. We now have to go out to people and talk to them, go and address parish councils and local community groups because that's —— philosophy and they keep winning the council seats . . .'
(E2)

The relationships between neighbourhood forums or community groups and elected members were not always so good. As previously mentioned there can be tensions between the voice of the elected representative of the area and the community. The relationship between neighbourhood forums and the democratic process was seen in one area 'as a mechanism of influencing the policy-maker rather than being policy-maker themselves' (H4). However, in the example of the tenant management organisation, councillors are on the board of the TMO. In another area councillors requested that nominations to the community health council be delegated to community action forum representatives (X2) as they were too busy. The fact that members are often part of the communities they represent, whereas officers may live outside the area, also means that they may understand their views more easily.

The impression gained from these parts of the discussions was that council officers have to be very sensitive to the nuances of the way their authority operates and the subtle balance of power and influence between committees, councillors, community groups and the executive, and to somehow juggle their relationships with other agencies, primarily health, alongside this. Their frustrations over the lack of recognition of these difficulties displayed by health partners were often apparent.

10. Measuring success

This chapter addresses four main groups of issues about information use, impact of services and evidence of effects:

- the access to and use of information by health authorities and local authorities and the potential for sharing management information
- indicators and measures in use and their limitations. Issues to do with measures of outputs versus long-term health gains and measures of quality
- engaging the interest of the community in indicators
- use of research and getting research evidence into practice.

Information-sharing between health and local authorities

Health authorities were considered to be generally better resourced in terms of access to information and skills in comparison to local authorities, and were better able to do health needs assessments. In one authority there had been joint arrangements to share resources for joint needs assessments on elderly health and mental health which had been felt to be successful, and as one respondent reported 'when we ask for [information] they are usually pretty helpful about trying to give it to us' (H5). This imbalance of information was particularly evident when joint health strategies were being developed. Health information on mortality and morbidity dominated draft strategies and pointed up where there were gaps where the local authority either did not have relevant information or had not thought to include it.

There was a feeling that health could be more interested in the types of information local authorities held, and could also help to inform service provision more effectively through health-based analysis of service outcomes. For example in environmental health:

'. . . if . . . a health-based analysis of the outcomes of our work said for example, you're spending too much time inspecting low-risk premises and not enough time inspecting high-risk premises, then I would say well, OK, thanks very much, that's very helpful . . . let's forget about the lowest ones because the actual health risk is minimal . . .' (E5)

There were clearly frustrations in not being able to engage in serious relevant epidemiological work themselves or to base work programmes on sound research information. There were also differences in the value placed on 'sound' by the different authorities. There had been examples of attempting to engage the health authority's superior information capacity in needs assessment work that would have been directly relevant to transportation issues and asthma, but:

'. . . we can never get a meeting of minds on this. Their perspective is far too academic. Again and again they just come back and say the results from that will be rubbish . . .' (E5)

Another way in which health authorities could help local authorities develop their information base to be more sensitive to health issues would be to help them audit their activities to see what health implications they have:

'I think what you would need . . . are people with a broad training with a health background actually working with each functional area of the local authority to analyse the potential of the health gain . . . so they have actually got the practical and viable things that engineers or housing experts can do linked with what they would like to achieve in health outcome terms.' (E1)

It was suggested that agencies did not do enough to share their information, not perhaps intentionally but simply because others did not know what was available, or only discovered it accidentally:

'We ought to . . . make some of our management information understandable to other organisations and we could all benefit from it.' (S3)

Indicators in use and their limitations

The majority of indicators in current use were either service delivery indicators or outputs, or customer satisfaction data. There was a wide range of quality information systems, such as continuous questionnaires, face-to-face discussions, feedback, customer comments books, etc. (L4), and more formal extensive survey methods conducted annually. Outcomes covered in these types of surveys related to items such as satisfaction with services: ' . . . are we dealing with your bins properly and car parking and what have you?' (E3). More open surveys about people's views of the city were also accessed through customer surveys and feedback panels, for example, specifically from young people to find out what they did or didn't rate about the city (L1). Service indicators related to monitoring of provision, for example, number of houses in which insulation had been installed (H2), but these were recognised as being intermediate, and inadequate to measure long-term effects on health.

The deficiencies in these measures were clear. For example, the whole area of measuring improvements in quality of life, which was often the aim of healthy city work, was impossible to assess by service indicators (S1). Similarly, the quality of service provision was not assessed by measures of inputs or services provided (H2). It is not possible to assess the health gain achieved over the long term and there are perverse incentives in the desire to get quick successes in joint work that bias reporting towards more immediate outcomes. On the other hand there was the sense that it did not matter whether the health benefit could be assessed if the actions could be justified in more traditional ways. In housing, for example:

> *'If we improve the thermal properties of our homes, it's warmer, asthma would be less, bronchial conditions and so forth and so we clearly see the health link. We have never needed or been able to actually quantify what that benefit is, frankly it's enough for us to know that it is beneficial . . . against the starting premise that it's good building maintenance anyway.'* (H1)

Indicators of the success of customer survey and user involvement methods were also suggested, such as setting targets for response levels to surveys and indicators of the perceived integration of services by, for example, clients understanding why they were visited by both a social worker and a district nurse.

Engaging community interest

Engaging the community's interest in indicators was seen to be important if authorities were going to create comprehensive sets of health and sustainability indicators. It was felt that these should encompass a wide range of environmental, social and educational indicators which should contain both a professional dimension and a community dimension. The professional dimension would be the baseline indicators, while it was felt that the community would be more interested in a subset of meaningful headline indicators to give a 'citizen's view of what is meant by health' (E1). Such headline indicators might reflect comparative performance with like authorities in the area that were known to local communities, and would need to be produced in a simplified user-friendly way. This would however need to be backed up by much fuller documentation of supporting measures, which would require close co-operation between authorities to produce an 'annual compendium of sustainability'. The goal was to:

> '. . . clear the clutter and to develop a logical rational set of indicators so that either this organisation or another organisation or a member of the public could see there's some logic to it.'
>   (E1)

There was however little indication in the authorities visited that much progress had been made in this direction.

Evidence-based practice

There were frequent mentions of lack of information on the effectiveness of services in terms of improving health, in housing, environmental health and social services. It was felt that the medical side of health had 'got its act together' (S2) with regard to evidence-based practice which was largely lacking in local authorities. Although examples were cited of occasional collaboration with research institutions to evaluate the effect of particular initiatives these were uncommon, and the impact of research on practice was slight:

> 'You can be in contact with all these research institutions but . . . the fact is a lot of it is pretty inaccessible and [for it] to be distilled into your own practice is the challenge . . .'
>   (H5)

This was an area in which most respondents were aware of the considerable gaps in their knowledge and the difficulties of closing them with good research information owing to lack of time and resources. Returning to the theme of closer collaboration on information-sharing with health authorities, it would appear that this is an area where the recognised skills of public health could help if there could be closer agreement on the value of different types of data and evaluation approaches, and the need to disseminate findings into practice.

11. Discussion

The respondents in the range of local authorities visited were generally enthusiastic in their concern for, and consideration of, the factors that promoted health in their communities, but were often frustrated in their attempts to take action by resource limitations, lack of political support and difficulties in working across agencies. Nevertheless an impressive array of actions was described by respondents across councils, and there were indications of a number of opportunities to consolidate and develop health-promoting work and partnerships.

Reducing inequalities

Local authorities felt that they had responsibility to promote the quality of life in its broadest sense, for their residents and for visitors, and considered that they were better positioned than health authorities to do this. Poor quality of life was seen to be associated with ill health through increased levels of stress, anxiety, depression, anti-social behaviour and social isolation. Both housing and social services departments saw that they had a role to play in improving the quality of life for the deprived or at-risk; while leisure and tourism services contributed to the improvement of the environment and the economy of the area as a whole. They also recognised the importance of thinking about positive health, both mental and physical and the wider wellbeing of people. This is in line with their roles as outlined in *Modern local government* (Department of the Environment, Transport and the Regions, 1998b) to promote the wellbeing of communities.

Reducing poverty and inequalities were seen as priorities for action, but although social services and housing departments were in contact with the poorer sections of the community there were indications that these opportunities were not always maximised to consider wider health needs. Provision of advice services enabled officers to address health issues underlying presenting problems in a reactive manner. In rural and more affluent areas the particular difficulties in focusing attention on inequalities were noted. There were also concerns about what seemed in some cases to be a lack of interest on the part of the health service in inequalities, and organisational problems in bringing agencies together to address these issues. However, there were also doubts about the value of targeting specific geographic areas with time-limited initiatives to redress inequalities. Negative effects of short-term project solutions included: enhancement of divisions in a community; reduction in community participation; loss of expertise of key workers at the end of projects; and perpetuating welfarism and dependency in the community.

While economic regeneration was seen as critical to improving health, and there were many examples of joint work over Single Regeneration Budget bids, the involvement of health and inclusion of health issues did not appear to be central in these considerations. The focus on the poorest neighbourhoods in the national strategy for neighbourhood renewal (Social Exclusion Unit, 1998) will only affect those councils with the most deprived areas. Although the approaches to be explored in the New Deal for Communities will provide a framework for the types of innovative work to tackle inequalities seen in this study, there are cautions about targeting communities and about difficulties in working with health partners that should be heeded.

Empowering communities

Local authorities have developed a variety of solutions to understanding the needs of communities better and to providing more responsive services. Discussions about community development indicated a lack of a clear distinction between community development as an approach or philosophy and as a council function. Community development was seen to be vital to make council services more aware of community concerns and to help develop self-esteem and self-sustaining communities. However, the arrangements for community development work were disparate and generally not integrated well with other council functions, and were under threat from resource cuts. There were however a number of ways in which authorities were seeking greater engagement with the community. These included community action forums, local ward committees, and advisory panels. The degree of engagement varied from consultation in public meetings, through local decision-making to delegated budgetary control. Ensuring adequacy of community representation was a concern and limitations to community representation in these types of forums were frequently mentioned.

The range of solutions and energy that appeared to be going into these approaches to understanding community needs and actively encouraging empowerment and involvement in this small sample was impressive, and echoed the range of approaches outlined by the Democracy Network (Local Government Association and Local Government Management Board, 1998). This guide to democratic practice describes various methods, from seeking the views of the public to creating public involvement and accountable and accessible local authorities. However the distinction between these types of approaches and community development was not clear. It appeared as though 'traditional' community development services were not always working closely with other mechanisms used to consult with and involve the community, and yet there are clear signs of the understanding of the potential of community empowerment. It would be useful to learn from the lessons of other community health initiatives and community building programmes to understand more about the different types of processes, their application and objectives, such as the Priority Estates Project in the UK (Gregory, 1998) and the Community Quality of Life Project in Canada (Raphael, Steinmetz and Renwick, 1998). Questions about how representative community mechanisms are, which methods are appropriate for what purposes and their achievements should be looked at in more detail. Clarity of purpose and clear communication of this to council members, staff and community participants is a key principle of developing democratic practice (LGA/LGMB, 1998).

While some community action approaches were clearly addressing health issues, these were not always labelled as such; thus issues to do with vermin and rubbish, or noise and transport, were seen as community concerns or quality of life issues rather than health ones. Opportunities afforded by the creation of networks of community groups appeared only rarely to be taken to consider health or health service issues. There appears to be untapped potential for using the extensive mechanisms established to address both broader health issues and for consultation on health service issues. It is suggested that health authorities should explore sharing these mechanisms with local authorities rather than attempting to duplicate them. Community development and participation approaches require resources to develop and sustain them and it would be prudent to share the costs. Also, experience suggests that the wider community tends to equate health issues more broadly with council services, while health service consultation is generally limited to user groups and pressure groups, and therefore these forums might provide a 'way in' for the NHS to consider wider health issues with the community.

Lessons learnt from joint working

Problems with joint working between departments in an authority and between health and the local authority were often described as being structural and organisational. NHS reorganisations, differences in approaches to contracting and target-setting and the plethora of groups engaged in planning were barriers to effective joint work. Other constraints included different perceptions of health, where it was felt that health services were more concerned with treatment issues than prevention. There was little engagement with GPs, and concerns that primary care group development work did not always involve the local authority. However, there were examples of good practice, and potential areas of joint work were proposed. Interdepartmental joint work was sometimes easier where the client group was similar. Respondents emphasised the importance of trust and expectation of reciprocity in relationships, honesty and realism in what could be achieved given the competing demands on everyone's agendas. The effect of the political dimension in local authorities needs further attention. There appears to be a gap in understanding the effects of the difference between health and local authorities in the way business is conducted, the relative freedom of officers to make decisions, and their democratic accountability, which creates tensions.

Work towards achieving joint health strategies seemed to be in its early stages in most areas, although there was optimism about this being the way forward. In particular there was a desire for a pragmatic approach to partnership work. While the benefits of an explicit strategy or policy was recognised, it was felt that strategic vision should not predominate, and that working together would be best achieved by focusing on practical, implementable action plans. The booklet *Health on the agenda* by the Health Education Authority and Local Government Management Board (1998) may be helpful for council staff and members in developing thinking along these lines.

The recent development of Health Improvement Programmes was causing some confusion. It was not clear at the time of the study whether these would look more like joint health strategies or purchasing plans. There was also little indication of collaboration on resources, except in limited project areas and for some joint posts, although the need seriously and openly to pool resources in order to deliver more effective services was clearly stated. This issue has been addressed with respect to pooling resources between health and social services in *Partnership in action* (Department of Health, 1998c), and changes in legislation and clarification of currently acceptable resource sharing will go some way to meeting these concerns.

Sharing information was another area in which it was felt that sharing resources would be of benefit. Public health departments in health authorities were seen to have superior information resources and skills, and while there were examples of good joint work on, for example, needs assessments, it was felt that there was potential for sharing more management information, and for support in critically considering their own data for health impact. However, differences in the perceived values of different types of data and research methods sometimes got in the way of collaborative working. Although there were some interesting ideas about useful indicators, and good examples of customer surveys, there had been little joint progress in this area. In particular there is little information on the effectiveness of services in health terms. Respondents would welcome the development of an evidence base and emphasised the importance of disseminating findings from research into practice.

When asked specifically about their experiences in Health for All or Healthy City projects, there was a general feeling that these had helped to put health on the agenda of the local authority and encouraged joint working between departments. However, there were limitations in the extent to which the alliances had been able to penetrate all parts of the authority and capture the interest of all departments. Health of the Nation had been a negative influence on some alliances because it had skewed the work towards individual behavioural change, which seemed less relevant to some local authority departments. Links between health and other strategic areas, anti-poverty, Agenda 21, etc. were only just beginning to be formed. There was also little indication of well-developed links between the extensive community engagement processes already described and health alliance work. The greatest successes in achieving good collaboration and community engagement were thought to be on tangible projects with visible outcomes. There was a very clear under-standing that developing alliances took time and considerable effort; and the experience of many was that it brought considerable benefits but that much remained to be done.

Recognising different types of partnership

From the descriptions of both successful and less successful joint working between departments and with the NHS, it became clear that there were tensions in engaging some partners to focus on some issues, and areas where it was relatively easy to cut across professional and organisational boundaries to promote health. Two distinct types of partnership seem to work best, one with a focus on clients and the delivery of appropriate and accessible services, and the second with a population focus.

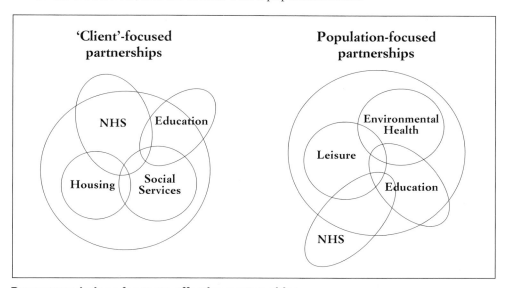

Recommendations for more effective partnerships

The relationships between agencies for client-focused and population-focused alliances are suggested in the figure. Many respondents described Maslow's (1943) hierarchy of needs and the difficulty of engaging individuals to aspire to higher levels of health when their basic requirements were not being adequately addressed. The successful initiatives to meet these needs were best delivered when there were close working relationships between the NHS, social services and housing departments targeted to a common client base. Partnerships with this focus were best able to address inequalities in health. Education services also have a part to play with respect to aspects of service provision for special needs children, educational welfare and school exclusions. The second focus for partnership work is the general population with a focus on geographically defined communities. Here there is the potential to address wider health concerns and primary prevention, where departments have ready access to the whole community through environmental health services, leisure and education. The NHS has a significant role to play here through public health information, health promotion services, primary care and community health services, but it is probably not a lead role.

This model is a simplification of the primary relationships but it might help to focus attention on where services can best make their contributions to promoting health, and who the major partners are for different types of action. Implicit in this model is the recognition that both approaches are of equal worth and that the synergy between them would help to meet community health promotion needs. Acknowledging this pattern of two types of partnership may help to deploy limited resources in a more targeted and relevant manner, and attempt to avoid the tensions and conflict that are experienced in working together when agencies have conflicting objectives.

However, the proposals for closer working between health and social services in *Partnership in action* (Department of Health, 1998c) do not currently include the option for housing services to be similarly integrated as this model proposes. Whilst the discussion document recognises the need for flexibility in working arrangements between the NHS and corporate local government that is beyond social services, further powers will be needed to enable this (Department of Health, 1998c). The leadership role given to local authorities (DETR, 1998b) would square with the suggestion that the NHS does not lead on wider population health issues. However, the NHS lead on Health Improvement Programmes, which would encompass preventive and public health aspects of National Service Frameworks, increases the complexity. Local authorities will be competing for 'Beacon Council' status, and yet this will probably be awarded on the basis of excellence in particular services (DETR, 1998b, para. 2.18), and the criteria for selection do not appear to include excellence in partnership arrangements. They are also tasked to develop a comprehensive strategy for promoting the wellbeing of their area and will need to ensure coherence with other local plans to which they contribute but which are led by other agencies, such as Health Improvement Programmes (DETR, 1998b, para. 8.16).

Whilst this raft of legislation is generally supportive of the directions in which most of these councils seem to want to go to promote community health, it does not fully address the problems of working in partnership across organisational boundaries all too familiar to those attempting to do so. In some ways, the policies may act to drive wedges further between organisations as the necessity to draw up different (albeit complementary) plans becomes more pressing.

Building social capital

This research has shown that local authorities understand their potential role in building social capital and are actively pursuing the objectives of improving residents' sense of community and quality of life. There is interest in understanding more about how these actions improve health but much remains to be done to develop appropriate measures of effectiveness in this area that would be acceptable to all parties. There were many examples of work that could be considered as contributing to promoting social capital, although they had not generally been conceived with that goal. There is a need to look more critically at the different objectives and approaches to assess their potential for community empowerment and how this might relate to the stated aims of consultation to improve service provision. From the perspective of local authorities the NHS appeared not to have exploited the opportunities afforded by such engagement, either to promote health or to consult on service provision. The contribution of the NHS to promoting social capital seems limited at this stage, and may best be made through focusing on congruent service provision to deprived and at-risk groups. There are, however, potential avenues for collaborative work to improve community health services to these groups and to support social support networks. Whilst the development of primary care groups and the Healthy Living Centre initiatives provided potential mechanisms for achieving this, at the time of the study there was little, if any, evidence that local authorities had been brought into the early planning stages of these developments.

The attributes of social capital building appear to be as relevant for the community of agencies working in partnership, as for the wider community. Effective partnerships were built on trust, expectation of reciprocity of actions and strong networks of contacts and information-sharing. Where there were deficits in these, partnerships were less effective or had broken down. In the absence of the statutory requirement on local authorities to deliver joint health strategies, these areas of work will continue to depend on goodwill, shared values and locally agreed forms of working. It would be helpful to do further work on the concept of social capital to learn more about how it can be developed both in the wider community and in intersectoral partnerships.

In conclusion, it appears that local authorities have much to contribute to the promotion of community health, but there is a need for the health service to understand these contributions more clearly, and to relinquish leadership for health promotion in areas where local authorities clearly have the edge and a lead responsibility. Constructing partnership arrangements with explicit and compatible objectives within an overall health strategy framework would reduce some of the frustrations inherent in current partnership working and allow services to contribute more effectively to the overall agenda. There is a need for further investigation and sharing of good practice between local authorities and health authorities in the areas of maximising the potential for health of community engagement arrangements, understanding the possibilities for developing social capital and developing common health and social indicators of success.

References

Department of Health (1997). *The new NHS: modern, dependable.* Cm 3807. London: Stationery Office.

Department of Health (1998a). *Our healthier nation: a contract for health.* Cm 3852. London: Stationery Office.

Department of Health (1998b). *Chief Medical Officer's project to strengthen the public health function in England: a report of emerging findings.* London: Department of Health.

Department of Health (1998c). *Partnership in action (new opportunities for joint working between health and social services): a discussion document.* http://www.open.gov.uk/doh/pia.htm

Department of the Environment, Transport and the Regions (1998a). *Modernising local government: local democracy and community leadership. a consultation paper.* London: Stationery Office.

Department of the Environment, Transport and the Regions (1998b). *Modern local government: in touch with the people.* Cm 4014. London: Stationery Office.

Environmental Health Commission (1997). *Agendas for change.* Chartered Institute of Environmental Health.

Gillies, P (1998). Effectiveness of alliances and partnerships for health promotion. *Health Promotion International* **13**(2): 99–120.

Gregory, S (1998). *Transforming local services: partnership in action.* York: Joseph Rowntree Foundation.

HEA and LGMB (1998). *Health on the agenda.* London: Local Government Management Board.

Higgins, D. *et al.* (1996). Social capital among community volunteers. The relationship to community level HIV programmes. *Abstracts of the VI International Conference on AIDS.* Vancouver. 2, 189 July.

Kawachi, I. *et al.* (1996). A prospective study of social networks in relation to total mortality and cardiovascular disease in men in the USA. *Journal of Epidemiology and Community Health* **50**: 245–51.

Local Government Association and Local Government Management Board (1998). *Democratic practice: a guide.* London: LGA Publications.

Maslow, A (1943). A theory of human motivation. *Psychological Review* **50**: 370–96.

Moran, G (1996). *Promoting health and local government.* London: HEA/LGMB.

Putnam, R D, Leonardi, R and Nanetti, R Y (1994). *Making democracy work: civic traditions in modern Italy.* Princetown: University Press.

Raphael, D, Steinmetz, B and Renwick, R (1998). *How to carry out a community quality of life project: a manual.* Ontario: University of Toronto.

Roberts, C and Griffiths, J (1998). *Picturing a healthy Wales: the health promoting role of local government.* Cardiff: Health Promotion Wales.

Social Exclusion Unit (1998). *Bringing Britain together: a national strategy for neighbourhood renewal.* Cm 4045. London: Stationery Office.

Wilkinson, R (1996). *Unhealthy societies: the afflictions of inequality.* London: Routledge.

World Health Organization (1986). *The Ottawa Charter: principles for health promotion.* Copenhagen: WHO Regional Office for Europe.

World Health Organization (1997). *The Jakarta Declaration on Health Promotion into the 21st century.* www.depkes.go.id/moment/jakdec.htm